D0167561

The MYTH of Romance

DENNIS McCALLUM
and
GARY DeLASHMUTT

BETHANY HOUSE PUBLISHERS
MINNEAPOLIS, MINNESOTA 55438

Published by Bethany House Publishers
A Ministry of Bethany Fellowship, Inc.
11300 Hampshire Avenue South
Minneapolis, Minnesota 55438

Printed in the United States of America.

Library of Congress Cataloging-in-Publication Data

McCallum, Dennis.
    The myth of romance : marriage choices that last a lifetime / Dennis
McCallum and Gary DeLashmutt.
        p.   cm.
    Includes bibliographical references.
    1. Marriage. 2. Marriage—Religious aspects—Christianity.
I. DeLashmutt, Gary, 1952-   . II. Title.
HQ734.M155   1996
248.8'44—dc20   96–4438
ISBN 1–55661–726–7   CIP

To our wives,

Holly and Bev,

who have graciously allowed us
to learn many of the lessons
in this book.

DENNIS McCALLUM is Senior Pastor at Xenos Christian Fellowship in Columbus, Ohio, and part of the Crossroads Project, a group conducting seminars on the postmodern challenge at universities across the country. He is the author of several books, including *Christianity: The Faith That Makes Sense, The Summons, The Death of Truth,* and *Walking in Victory.*

GARY DeLASHMUTT is Co-Senior Pastor at Xenos Christian Fellowship in Columbus, Ohio. He is the author of *Loving God's Way,* and a contributing author in *The Death of Truth.* He has been married to Bev for eighteen years.

CONTENTS

ONE

MARRIAGE SUCCESS TODAY: WHAT ARE YOUR CHANCES?

They dream in courtship, but in wedlock wake.

—ALEXANDER POPE

Marriage is like twirling a baton, turning handsprings, or eating with chopsticks. It looks easy till you try it.

—HELEN ROWLAND

There is a lot to get used to in the first year of marriage. One wakes up in the morning and finds a pair of pigtails on the pillow that were not there before.

—MARTIN LUTHER

Kim and Jay were like so many other couples when we met them. Before getting married they had lived together for over a year in a trial marriage. But it didn't help. After several years of stormy marriage, they were separated again. First Jay, and later Kim, began attending home Bible studies in our area. Within a month both met Christ personally.

As they learned to build trust in their new Christian friends, each recounted with tears the soul-numbing pain they had inflicted on each other during their failed effort to forge a lasting relationship. They struggled with their relationship for months, eventually undergoing counseling. Finally they were reunited.

Things didn't go smoothly, especially at first. But today, thirteen years later, they are still married, well-adjusted, and now have three beautiful children and a powerful Christian ministry. Their former addictions and unfaithfulness are nowhere in sight. Jesus Christ changes lives.

As our culture hurtles downward into marital failure and despair, couples like Kim and Jay are headed the opposite direction—toward marital success. As postmodern culture opts for lonely autonomy, unqualified freedom, and cheap thrills, others are finding the mystery and contentment of union with another.

A union relationship: It's God's answer to loneliness.

God's Pattern

In Genesis 2:24, God decreed that a man and woman should "leave" their parents and "cleave" to each other, and the two "shall become one flesh." This union of two distinct individuals is what we call marriage. Such a union relationship involves much more than procreation, although children are certainly a wonderful expression of the oneness of husband and wife. Thousands of years later, both Jesus and Paul quoted this very text when explaining the essence of sex and marriage. (See Matthew 19:5 and 1 Corinthians 6:16.) These passages both confirm that a union relationship, as described in Genesis 2, is God's central idea for marriage.

As people created in the image of God, we all desire the experience of union in a relationship and the sense of completion that comes with it. We can see this need illustrated in Genesis 2. Shortly after Adam's creation, God showed him the animals because, as God said, "It is not good for the man to be alone" (v. 18). On one level, Adam wasn't alone. After all, he was surrounded by God's creatures. But God brought the animals to Adam to teach him something important about his humanity. The man learned that none of the animals was "a helper corresponding to him" (v. 20, NASB, literal marginal rendering). In other words, Adam could not experience real unity with anything but another personal being like himself.

Today, the need for union in relationships is as central to being human as it ever was. Without union relationships we feel incomplete and lonely. We learn from the New Testament that God meets our desire for union first by uniting us with himself through our faith in Jesus Christ (1 Corinthians 6:17). This union relationship with God is his foundational answer to loneliness and alienation. When we are united with Christ, then we can also experience substantial union in relationships with other Christians because of the union of believers in the body of Christ. (See Romans 12:5 and John 17:21. We will give a complete explanation of this teaching in Chapter 4.)

Many also have the opportunity to experience the oneness of marriage—a union so real that it demonstrates the union of Christ and the Church in a unique way (Ephesians 5:28–32). Single Christians are rightly excited about the prospect of experiencing such a relationship.

> God meets our desire for union first by uniting us with himself, and then with other believers.

Do you want to succeed in marriage? If so, you've come to the right place! This book began as material primarily intended to help single Christians get off to a good start in marriage, even if marriage lies years in the future. If you are single, we will explore important choices you can make *before* marriage that will help you forge a successful union. For those of you who are already married, this book will help you move ahead to build lasting unity in your relationships while working on your current problems.

Whether single or married, we are all making choices today that will affect our future. How can we know which ones are right? Let's examine together how to evaluate our choices according to God's timeless standards, and how to avoid the pitfalls of postmodern thought about marriage and romance.

Marriage in the Late Twentieth Century

Unfortunately, the Western world is profoundly unsuccessful at marriage. Although in the 1990s more people than ever are getting married, divorce is keeping pace. America has the highest divorce rate in the world. Today, half as many are divorced every year as are married. People seem to feel their need for a deep and lasting love relationship more strongly than ever, but at the same time they are further than ever from success.

Single Christians, on the other hand, are in an excellent position to build successful marriages. As Christians we have the basis and the power to do so, but first we must decisively reject the secular approach to marriage choices and build instead on a solid scriptural foundation.

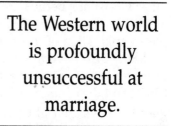

The Western world is profoundly unsuccessful at marriage.

In the past, the evangelical Christian community was largely immune to the heavy divorce trend in society, but today this is no longer true. Recent studies show that people in the Christian community are also beginning to fail at marriage.[1] Two factors have contributed strongly to this disturbing trend.

Media Bombardment

The *unprecedented multimedia attack on the biblical view of sexuality* has contributed to marriage failure during the past three decades. People now reaching marrying age have been raised under the influence of TV, cinema, music, and literature that, with rare exceptions, deny the biblical role of sex. In its place, these sources advance a casual, self-centered view of sex. They usually promote self-gratification as the primary goal in a sexual relationship. According to the media consensus of our day, anyone who gives up any possible pleasure has made a foolish compromise.

Even young children sustain a daily barrage of claims that

the key to happiness is a selfish sexual relationship. This media bombardment, which usually includes no Christian alternative, affects children who lack the critical faculty to evaluate such claims. Christian parents face a challenge today as they try to impart to their children the ability to think critically and biblically about the material on TV and other media.

Emotional and Relational Poverty

The second factor contributing to the increasing failure in marriage is the *emotional and relational poverty* fostered in existing modern Western families. Materialistic priorities in family life lead to extended work hours and two-income families, even when the family could make it on one income. The result is reduced parental availability to children and a corresponding rise in later adjustment problems. At UCLA in 1992, in a disturbing study of over 400 infants, toddlers, and preschoolers, researchers found that "young children feel less secure with a teacher in a daycare center than with their own mother." Contrary to what many would expect, they found no correlation between the length of time children were with a teacher and their security scores. They concluded that even long-term, stable daycare is not a fully adequate substitute for a mother.[2]

The rising divorce rate also tends to perpetuate itself because children of divorce are less likely to form, or even to seek, lasting marriages. In a study of 11,000 adults conducted at Albany N.Y. State University in 1992, researchers found that, compared to those who had lived with only one parent, adults who had lived with both parents were more likely to agree that it is better to marry, that marriage is for life, and that kids are better off living with their parents. Adults who had never lived with their father were particularly likely to reject traditional social norms.[3] Another recent study of 340 freshmen at Auburn found that students from divorced families had lower scores on a "Favorableness of Attitude Toward Marriage Scale" questionnaire than did peers from intact families.[4] Both of these studies suggest the same thing: Broken marriages not only decrease children's *ability* to build good families, but also reduce their *desire* to do so.

Absentee parents and illegitimacy are growing problems in America. Decreased nurture and guidance at home often lead to insecurity and lack of self-control in adolescents and young adults. Recent studies have shown that teens missing a parent at home are more likely to get involved in sexual activity and substance abuse.[5] This lack of self-discipline can be a serious hindrance in establishing sacrificial relationships, which require consistent effort, often without immediate reward. Young people with low frustration tolerance find it difficult to succeed in marriage where disciplined, self-giving love is the only lasting foundation.

Even though these problems are severe, they are not hopeless. God's power is great, and he can change even the most damaged lives. But it isn't easy, and it won't happen without our active cooperation.

Preparation Is Critical

For all of these reasons, greater preparation is essential before attempting marriage today. Because of the intense pressure against marriage in the modern world, insufficient maturity can be disastrous. In an environment of near starvation, only the strong survive. Today, unfortunately, only the spiritually and emotionally strong marriages survive.

Maybe in earlier eras, people could simply find someone they felt love for and get married. Today, succeeding at marriage is less like walking next door and more like climbing a mountain. You wouldn't set out to climb a mountain without any planning or preparation, and if you did, you would probably get a nasty surprise. This isn't to say mountain climbing is bad. Actually it can be a great experience, but the ill-prepared and ill-equipped usually don't enjoy it much. They can, in fact, freeze to death on the mountainside. So, too, marriage success requires preparation in advance.

Some marriages, of course, flourish without any consciously

biblical underpinnings. But these are the exceptions. Today, the number of failures is so high that undertaking marriage based on the belief that "We'll be different" is like playing Russian roulette. Few of us would be willing to play such a dangerous game. The chances of dying are one in six—far too high for any responsible person! But have you considered that the risks involved in a secular marriage are even worse? Based on today's trends, couples lunging into marriage without a strong spiritual basis have not one, but as many as three of the gun's six chambers loaded with deadly bullets. Non-Christians who marry today are more likely than not to encounter the worst experience of their lives—an experience so terrible they may never fully escape its consequences in this life.

God's Will and Your Choices

Some young Christians think that just because they are Christians, God won't allow them to get into serious trouble in marriage. This simply is not true. As Christians, we are responsible for the use of our free will, even when we may not realize how important our choices are.

When Christians experience the negative consequences of their poor choices, they sometimes ask, "Why does God allow me to suffer in this situation instead of changing it for the better?" As pastors and counselors, we hear this plea more often in connection with miserable marriages than anything else. The pain that people, including Christians, experience from marital disappointment can be one of the most intense and lasting types of suffering. Those in despair feel as though God has abandoned them.

But if God always changed the situation we chose, our choices would have no significance at all, would they? We could choose anything knowing that—right or wrong—God would always straighten out the results for us. This amounts to a separation of free choice from responsibility. Is it reasonable to say that whatever we choose, God is responsible for the outcome? The Bible denies this idea.

Hebrews 12:16–17 reminds us of a shocking incident from the Old Testament, the story of Esau's free choice. In this story Esau, Isaac's firstborn son, had the legal right to inherit his father's estate. His father not only owned some property, but also the rights to a special covenant with God: namely, the privilege to be used by God in a unique way as his chosen family.

Esau came home from an unsuccessful hunting trip one day and found his younger brother Jacob cooking some soup. Esau was so hungry he was willing to do anything to get some. Seizing this opportunity, Jacob offered him the soup in exchange for his inheritance rights. In a moment, Esau agreed and sold his inheritance for a single meal. (See Genesis 25:27–34.)

Years later, Esau realized this was a mistake and tried to reverse the decision (or "repent" as Hebrews 12:17 says). But we read: ". . . afterwards, when he desired to inherit the blessing, he was rejected, for he found no place for repentance, though he sought for it with tears." Esau could still receive God's forgiveness for his wrong choice, but his birthright was forever lost—even though he begged his father with tears to restore it to him.

Does it seem cruel that Esau's life was forever affected by a bad decision he made on an impulse? After all, he was extremely hungry when he made the decision. Yet, this is the nature of free choice. The decisions we make are important—even to the extent that they can permanently change our lives. This is true even if we, like Esau, do not realize the importance of the decision at the time we make it.

> No hunger is so severe that it justifies trading away God's will to satisfy it.

The story also stands as a warning: There is no such thing as a hunger so severe that it justifies trading away God's will in order to satisfy it.

Both of these lessons apply directly to dating and marriage. Christians sometimes feel that their need for romantic love is so strong they cannot put up with the time and preparation required for a biblically based relationship. Some respond by engaging in sexual immorality as a quick pathway to love. Others insist on getting married even though they lack the maturity necessary for success. Of course, we can err and still be accepted by God. But we cannot assume that God will later step in and remove the consequences of our actions.

Sometimes God, in his grace, does change the bitter outcomes of our bad choices, as he did for Kim and Jay. As a result, some very painful marriages eventually become quite satisfying. But God will not do so without our cooperation and a willingness to learn. A bad marriage can recover when a couple learns to stop making poor decisions. Although the couple realizes they're in trouble, they stick with each other, trying to learn and practice God's will. Eventually, they find themselves entering into a rewarding relationship.

This is not to say that God is in favor of our making wrong choices so that he can step in later and "fix" them. He does not give us a blank check to do what we want without danger. There is a difference between God's ability to bring good out of disaster—his redemptive power—and God's moral will. It is so much easier and more productive to do his will in the first place than to have to learn through our mistakes. Many people, including Christians, who have been through deep suffering in their marriages report that the pain they endure in marriage can be even worse than that in single life. Most wish they had taken additional time to prepare for their marriages. Couples who have struggled through a painful marriage to the point of success are usually the strongest voices warning against careless and godless marriage choices.

Informed Free Choice

Jean Paul Sartre, an atheist, laments that man is totally responsible for his decisions, even though he has no way of knowing what the consequences of those decisions will be. One doesn't have to be an existentialist philosopher to feel that our moral choices are stabs in the dark. But, as Christians, we reject

17

this viewpoint.[6] There are, of course, some decisions we have to make with no way of knowing what the outcome will be. For instance, we don't know what will happen when we decide to have children. Some may be born with serious birth defects. Some may fall in with the wrong crowd. In these cases, we trust God to give us grace to overcome adversity and pain. Marriage choices, however, do not fall entirely into the category of the unknowable. As we shall see, we do have some concrete ways of knowing whether a marriage will work.

When suffering occurs in marriage, many Christians are tempted, like their non-Christian peers, to avoid their responsibility through divorce. But the emotional scars resulting from divorce can create equally permanent suffering. No one knows this better than divorcés and those who grew up in broken homes. Even though there may be some situations where divorce is the lesser evil, no Christian should enter marriage entertaining divorce as an option.

Christians seeking to avoid responsibility for bad decisions often plead that they were ignorant when they made the decision. "I was practically a child!" cries the unhappy wife or husband. "God should let me off the hook!" But ignorance of God's will doesn't remove responsibility. Even when we make mistakes based on ignorance, we usually bear the consequences because this is how God teaches us not to be ignorant. Otherwise, ignorance would be the ideal

> Ignorance of God's will doesn't remove responsibility.

state. Instead, the apostle Paul adjures us, "So then, do not be foolish, but understand what the will of the Lord is" (Ephesians 5:17).

Because of the real dangers in choosing the right time and person to marry, a healthy respect for the importance of the decision is only reasonable. We may lightly decide what clothes to wear in the morning, but only a fool ignores the awesome implications of the choice to marry. By the same token, the satisfaction we can experience in a solid Christian marriage is difficult to imagine. You can earn a dollar by shining someone's shoes, but if you want to earn $10,000 you have to do much more than that. Marriage is worth far more than $10,000, and it may take still more work and self-sacrifice if we want complete success.

If you get married, you will either enter a cauldron of pain and confusion you never imagined possible, or you will use the relational and spiritual tools you gained before marriage to grow out of your problems by drawing on the power of God. Even if you're already married, it's not too late. You will have to learn now, within marriage, the things you should have learned before marriage. It may be harder this way, but it's possible, and God will help you. Why not resolve now to give God a chance to help you, by reading and praying through the rest of this short book? You'll be glad you did.

It's exciting to realize that by taking some down-to-earth measures, you can be confident that your marriage will work. A strong Christian marriage, in turn, will become a solid base for your emotional and spiritual life. God will use your marriage to fashion your character as nothing else can. In the end, marriage, like other challenges in your life, will help to conform you to the image of Christ. (See Romans 8:29–30.)

Notes

1. William M. Kinard, "Divorce and Remarriage: Ministers in the Middle," and Jim Smoke, "Pastoring the Divorced: Caring Without Condoning," both in *Christianity Today*, Vol. 24 (June 6, 1980).
2. Howes and Hamilton, "Children's Relationships With Caregivers: Mothers and Child Care Teachers," *Child Development*, Vol. 63 (1992), pp. 859–866.
3. Katherine Trent and Scott J. South, "Sociodemographic Status, Parental Background, Childhood Family Structure, and Attitudes Toward Fam-

ily Formation," *Journal of Marriage and Family*, Vol. 54 (1992), pp. 427–439.

4. Jennings, Salts, and Smith, "Attitudes Toward Marriage: Effects of Parental Conflict, Family Structure, and Gender," *Journal of Divorce and Remarriage*, Vol. 17 (1992), pp. 57, 78.

5. A major study of 1500 adolescents conducted by the University of Arkansas and the University of Maryland in 1991 demonstrated a higher likelihood of fornication among teens who were missing one parent at home. See Benda and Blasio, "Comparison of Four Theories of Adolescent Sexual Exploration," *Deviant Behavior*, Vol. 12 (1991), pp. 235–257. In another study of over 80,000 high school students nationwide, the researchers found a striking correlation between family structures and abuse of marijuana, cocaine, alcohol, and other drugs. Specifically, children missing one parent were far more likely to abuse drugs. This correlation held true even when the researchers controlled for economic, educational, regional, and urban-rural variables. See John M. Wallace, Jr. and Jerald G. Buchanan, "Explaining Racial/Ethnic Differences in Adolescent Drug Use: The Impact of Background and Lifestyle," *Social Problems*, Vol. 38 (1991), pp. 333–352. In another study conducted by Columbia University and the New York Psychiatric Institute in 1992, the researchers found that "The incidence of substance abuse in offspring was associated with parental divorce." They found that children of divorce had "seven times the risk for developing substance abuse disorder" than did children of intact families. See Myrna Weissman et al., "Incidence of Psychiatric Disorder in Offspring at High and Low Risk for Depression," *Journal of the American Academy of Child and Adolescent Psychiatry*, Vol. 31 (1992), pp. 640–648. Similar results have been noted with problem drinking. See David R. Foxcroft and Geoff Lowe, "Adolescent Drinking Behavior and Family Socialization Factors: A Meta-Analysis," *Journal of Adolescence*, Vol. 14 (1991), pp. 255–273.

6. For a discussion of the existentialist perspective, see Jean Paul Sartre, trans. by Bernard Frechtman, *Existentialism* (New York: Philosophical Library, 1947), pp. 11–34.

TWO

Is "Love" Enough?

Where both deliberate, the love is slight:
Who ever lov'd, that lov'd not at first sight?

—CHRISTOPHER MARLOWE

Before marriage, a man will lie awake thinking about something you
said; after marriage, he'll fall asleep before you finish saying it.

—HELEN ROWLAND

Every pastor or counselor working with young married couples is familiar with certain unhappy refrains:

"He used to comfort me—now he acts indifferent when I'm upset."
"She always stayed thin when we were dating. Look at her now."
"I don't feel like he's really interested in what I'm thinking and feeling."
"She was so agreeable before we got married. Where did all these strong opinions come from?"

What are these people saying? Are we at the mercy of chance, hoping our spouse doesn't change into someone we never would have married? God has the answers.

Love and Marriage

Most people hope their marriages will be based on love, but not everyone agrees on what the word "love" means. The Bible recognizes several kinds of love, but it insists that one specific type of love is essential in a good marriage. Jesus and the apostles chose a little-used Greek word to emphasize that Christian love is different than other types of love. The word they used most often for this special kind of love is *agape*.[1]

> Husbands, love (*agapao*) your wives . . . (Ephesians 5:25).
> "A new commandment I give to you, that you love (*agapao*) one another, even as I have loved you . . ." (John 13:34).

Agape is easily confused with other types of love that will not properly sustain marriage. We will use the term "Christian love" to refer to this special Christlike love, not because Christians can't love in other ways, but because this is the love that is essential to a biblical marriage. The apostle John explains:

> We know love by this, that He laid down His life for us; and we ought to lay down our lives for the brethren. But whoever has the world's goods, and beholds his brother in need and closes his heart against him, how does the love of God abide in him? (1 John 3:16–17).

According to this passage, Christian love is not based primarily on emotion. Rather, a working definition should look like this:

Christian love is a voluntary commitment to give of yourself in every area to meet the appropriate needs of another person.

When asked about loving one's neighbor, Jesus told the story of the Good Samaritan (Luke 10:30–37). The Samaritan found a badly wounded man and bandaged his wounds before picking him up and putting him on his donkey. He then took him to an inn and paid for him to recuperate there for a week. This, Jesus said, was an example of loving others. The Samaritan felt compassion for the wounded man, so feelings were involved. Now, for all we know, the Levite and the scribe—who had earlier passed by and had left the man in the road—also felt compassion for him. The difference is that the Samaritan actually *did* something sacrificial. He gave of himself (time, effort, and money) to meet the man's needs.

When the apostle John refers to giving our money to a needy person, he is not just describing a feeling we have for that person. Neither is "laying down our lives" a feeling (judging from what Christ did at the Cross). Laying down our lives is an *action*; it is something we either do or do not do, regardless of how we feel. One day we may have a warm, affectionate feeling toward a loved one; the next day we may not. Yet Christian love would choose to serve the other person on either day, not because it feels good, but because it is the will of God. Such love is the fulfillment of a commitment.

In addition to commitment, mature Christians have learned that, in the long run, their own feelings of love will grow most from a way of life based on self-giving Christian love. That's right. Selfless love is not only the *result* of spiritual growth and maturity, it is also an important *cause* of growth.

> Selfless love is not only the *result* of spiritual growth, it is also an important *cause* of growth.

Those who have learned to consistently practice Christian love derive satisfaction from the act of giving itself. Jesus, referring to the effect of self-giving love, said, "I have food to eat that you know nothing about" (John 4:32, NIV). He fed his spirit through the serving love he practiced with the Samaritan woman when he offered her God's love. This is also what Jesus meant when he said, "It is more blessed [e.g. "enriching"] to give than to receive" (Acts 20:35). We can experience feelings commonly associated with *receiving* love when we develop a taste for *giving* love sacrificially. In fact, if we set out with a goal of receiving love feelings we usually end up dissatisfied. Only when we look away from our own emotional needs (trusting God to meet them) and move out to meet others' needs will our own needs be fully met.

Beth was an unhappy young woman who experienced repeated failure in personal relationships. In a series of counseling sessions, she often complained about the way she was being treated by others. It seems people never loved her the way they should. She was bitterly disappointed in the shallow love others showed for her, and their failure to recognize her needs. She had been widowed after a short marriage, but before her first husband died, he had failed the test as well.

After a number of sessions where we studied the Bible on the subject of Christian love, Beth gradually became convinced from the heart that the real problem might be her outlook on love. She decided to try a new approach to her friendships: Instead of judging whether her friends were showing the kind of love they should, she would begin to focus only on whether she had victoriously given of herself for their good.

No instantaneous change occurred. But after several years, she stood to share her testimony at a Christian meeting. She told how she had lived in constant disappointment when she used to focus on her need to be loved. Now, she shared, she had learned the power of self-giving love. She had rewarding friendships, and her second marriage was as victorious as her first had been barren. The difference? Not that her new husband was better at loving her, but that she now knew the joy of giving of herself. Ironically, her husband and friends did seem more loving toward her, largely because they perceived her as a lovable person rather than a demanding love-taker.

Jesus said, "For whoever wants to save his life will lose it, but whoever loses his life for me will save it" (Luke 9:24, NIV). This is the mystery of selfless love. The Bible tells us that only a lifestyle characterized by practicing Christian love will be truly fulfilling. Jesus frequently taught this seemingly paradoxical concept to his disciples. (See John 13:12–17; 15:10–12; and Luke 9:24.)

Although the term "Christian love" is not primarily describing a feeling, neither is it incompatible with feelings, nor divorced from feelings. When we set out to meet needs in others, we realize emotional needs are often among their most intense personal needs. Mature lovers have learned to work with their loved ones to meet such deep inner needs at least part of the time.

Romance and Marriage

Many Christian couples believe they are practicing Christian love with each other during their dating relationship when, in fact, they are not. This becomes evident when, sooner or later after getting married, their love seems to desert them. Such couples are usually confused and depressed by the change. Some engage in recriminations, claiming their spouses have changed. Others blame themselves, falsely concluding that they have chosen the "wrong" mate, and so are doomed to futility. But the real problem is that they have not been expressing mature Christian love.

In a popular song, the lyricist complains that he keeps "falling in and out of love" with the same girl.[2] Mature Christian love-based relationships are free from this problem. Since Christian love is a voluntary, or willful, commitment to give, it is not subject to momentary feelings. Therefore, we cannot "fall out" of Christian love as if it were beyond our control. We don't "fall in" Christian love either. Instead, we have to *build into* a Christian love relationship.

> We don't "fall in" Christian love. Instead, we have to *build into* a Christian love relationship.

The kind of love we can—and invariably do—fall out of is what the Greeks called *eros*. *Eros* was defined by the Greeks as "the passion that overwhelms," and it corresponds to our modern concept of romantic love.[3] When emotions of attraction and desire for another person suddenly well up from within, we say we have "fallen in love." Such an emotional experience usually occurs involuntarily and sometimes instantaneously. Therefore, people even speak of "love at first sight."

25

In our culture, falling in (*eros*) love is certainly the main, if not the only, criterion for marriage choices. Using this standard, a couple can justify even the most hazardous marriage plans with the plea, "But we're in love!" The concept is so ingrained in modern culture that even strong Christians find themselves asking, "How do I know when it's really love?" Such a question reveals that they believe in a romantic attraction so powerful that nothing can change it. They think the key to success is making sure they find "true" love—*eros* so true it will never fade.

Once married, many are shocked when this kind of love dissipates. Suddenly, they look at their spouses and feel not "the passion that overwhelms" but something more like bland indifference or even, at times, aversion. When this happens, today's social norm is to admit they made a mistake, get a divorce, and try again. Unfortunately, we can safely predict that the same cycle will repeat itself all over again—until they change their minds about what kind of love is foundational in marriage.

Myth Versus Reality

There is no such thing as a "true" love that will indefinitely sustain a strong sensation of romantic excitement. Humans, by nature, are unable to sustain such a prolonged intense emotional experience. Romantic feelings tend to come and go. Sometimes married people even find themselves unintentionally "falling in love" with someone other than their own spouse! This can be quite confusing to those who view romantic love as the key to decision making in marriage. What's a Christian to think when this happens?

Interestingly, even though the concept of *eros* was deeply ingrained in Greek culture, the New Testament never mentions it. This fact strongly suggests that "falling in love" should not be the primary basis for deciding whom and when to marry. As Christians, we should emphatically reject the dangerous modern myth that "I will get married when I fall in love because it will last forever."

Today, many lifelong believers in the romance myth have been forced by harsh experience to question its validity. Many people refuse to get married because they fear their romantic feelings will desert them if they do. Instead, they live together in uncommitted relationships and suffer the insecurities and spiritual bruising of uncommitted sexual love. The last twenty-five years have witnessed an unprecedented increase in cohabitation.

Many who choose to cohabit believe that these "trial marriages" will enhance their chances for success in marriage. By living together, they will be able to finally determine whether or not their love is "the real thing." The actual results couldn't be further from modern expectations. Cohabitation *decreases* the likelihood of success in marriage, and the longer a couple cohabits, the *more* likely they are to fail in marriage. As Christians, we know that any solution that directly violates the will of God will fail. The Bible is clear that fornication is a dreadful betrayal of the Lord and of the one we misuse in this way, not to mention our own selves. No wonder trial marriages don't work.

According to a study at Johns Hopkins and the University of Wisconsin in 1992, "Cohabiting unions are much less stable than [unions] that begin as marriages." They found that 40 percent of cohabiting unions end before marriage. Of those relationships making it as far as marriage, divorce is much more

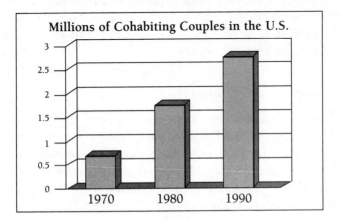

27

likely than for couples who did not cohabit. Approximately 75 percent of these marriages end in divorce. As a result, the researchers found that only 15 percent of cohabiting relationships will result in lasting marriage.[4] With chances of success in marriage running as low as one in two in the society as a whole, by cohabiting with a lover, you reduce your chances of marital success to one in seven!

This finding is contradictory to modern theories about what makes for successful love relationships, but it accords exactly with the view found in the Bible. Cohabitation studies confirm that the romance ideal is pure myth. Cohabitation not only results in greater likelihood of divorce, it also assures lower quality in the marital relationship itself.[5]

Divorce rates have remained high with only insignificant temporary fluctuations. This incidence continues in spite of the more than three-fold increase in cohabitation, and does not include the millions of breakups that never appear in the divorce statistics. Even if we were among the lucky ones who didn't get divorced, we would be doing serious damage to ourselves spiritually by following the bankrupted course of the world in the area of love. Considering these facts, why would we, as Christians, entrust our marital futures to the world's romance myth?

> By cohabiting with a lover, you reduce your chances of marital success to one in seven!

The Inadequacy of *Eros*

The problem with marriage today is that there is no foundation for it other than *eros*. Although there is nothing wrong with romantic love, it is entirely inadequate as a basis for a permanent life commitment. We may have no personal objections to car CD players, but they alone are an inadequate basis for travel. If we want to travel, we may want a CD player, but we also need a vehicle to put it in! The vehicle is the most important part of the whole equation—the central thing we need for travel.

Likewise, Christian love rather than *eros* is the central thing we need in marriage. Like first-century man, for whom *eros* was the basis of mystery religions, modern man has believed in a mystical love notion as the basis for marriage. In both cases, *eros* has proven to be inadequate. If, on the other hand, our marriages are based on Christian love and the principles of God's Word, they will not fail.

"Love . . . bears all things . . . endures all things. Love never fails" (1 Corinthians 13:4, 7–8).

Discerning *Eros*

How can you know if you are being influenced excessively by the romance myth in your dating or marriage choices? Here are a few indicators:

- If you ever ask the question "Is my love for my partner 'the real thing'?" it strongly suggests you believe in the *eros* myth described above. There is no answer to such a question because there is no such thing as "the real" *eros* love in the sense the word is being used here. This question implies that if your love is real, it will not fade in the future. Yet this feeling, like all feelings, will fade at times.

  The usual answer to this question is, "You'll know when it happens, so if you're still asking, it hasn't happened yet." This self-validating answer is untrue and misleading. Christians should consider the fact that this teaching is simply not found in the Bible. What a startling omission this would be in God's Word if such a love were the true basis for marriage! On the contrary, the Bible does give us detailed information on the nature of true Christian love and how to practice it. Today, many young Christians are engaging in an unfruitful search for "real" love instead of developing the basic relational skills they will need in marriage. Others, already in a struggling marriage, are wasting time looking for

29

lost *eros* feelings, or even becoming involved in erotic extra-marital affairs instead of setting about the task of learning to love as Christ loved us.

- When considering the reasons for wanting to marry or date someone, what comes to your mind most prominently? Is it a movement of his eyes? A memory of her body? The scent of her hair? The warm feeling you get when you're near him? These criteria all fall into the category of the erotic and, as such, are unrelated to the issue of Christian love. This is not to say they are incompatible with Christian love, but they should not be confused with it. If these areas of attraction are your sole, or even your main, criteria for marriage, it suggests that romance is your final guide to marriage decisions. Have you considered that virtually every divorced couple in Western society probably felt the same sense of *eros* attraction for the one they eventually divorced?

  Likewise, when we judge the quality of our existing marriage by the presence or absence of strong romantic love of this kind, disappointment is sure to follow. We would be judging our marriage by a standard alien to the Bible and contrary to the way God made us. Before long, those who rely on *eros* as their standard for marital happiness will find other people who can deliver *eros* on a level their spouse cannot. The resulting adultery proves nothing except that we should have gone by God's standards to begin with.

- Do others complain that you are dropping your friendships and responsibilities? "You're never around anymore!" Of course, some of your friends might be jealous, or your co-workers or bosses might be too picky. But, especially if you hear this kind of feedback from different sources, you should take heed. *Eros* is like a strong narcotic, and unless you have the maturity to exercise self-control, it tends to usurp other important areas of your lives. And because it is so pleasurable, those under its sway find it easy to rationalize their critics as people who "just don't understand what it means to be in love." For this reason, dating couples should make a commitment to each other to stay involved with their friends and to keep up with their school, work, and ministry responsibilities. They should also carefully consider criticism in this area and be willing to decrease time together if this problem arises.

- Do you tend to become very intimate with your dating partner in a short period of time? This usually means you are experiencing *eros*—a pleasurable, even thrilling experience. But it can also create an illusion of intimacy: Strong feelings of attraction lead us to believe we have found our soul mate, when in fact we hardly know each other. On this shaky foundation, couples initiate increasing intimacy to perpetuate and deepen their romantic feelings for one another. But many forms of intimacy are dangerous in a new dating relationship when we have no way of knowing whether the relationship will progress or fail. Sexual intimacy, of course, should be reserved for marriage, as we shall see later. In addition, wise Christians are cautious when talking about the relationship—how great it would be to be married, how much we love each other, how badly we want to be together—because we could easily be projecting implied promises that tend to build a momentum of their own. We end up feeling pressured to move ahead even if we sense it may be unwise. Some kinds of intimacy should be reserved for much later in a relationship after it has demonstrated real maturity and health.

- Are you unable to articulate your dating partner's weaknesses? Do your friends say you react with excessive defensiveness to those who offer a criticism? Couples who are "in love" often say that because they never fight or disagree their love is the "real thing." *Eros* is notoriously blind to a lover's weaknesses, and those under its spell tend to respond with outrage to any who poke holes in their idealized image of the other person. Some Christians spiritualize this blindness by claiming that God has "shown them" he approves of their relationship in spite of overwhelming objective evidence that they are in trouble. By contrast, dating couples who are forging a relationship based on Christian

31

love temper their feelings of attraction with realism. They will not feel compelled to ignore or defend their partner's character weaknesses, because their love is a commitment to do good to the other person rather than an emotional state to be maintained at all costs. They make constructive criticism, along with encouragement, a part of their relationship from the beginning.

The *Eros* Myth in History

Eros is a powerful and enjoyable experience. It would be wrong to repress all feelings of romance or to suggest that *eros* is carnal or evil. The Song of Solomon, for instance, is a celebration of romantic love. In fact, for most in modern Western society, *eros* is a prerequisite for marriage. Our romantic expectations today mean that an absence of a good level of *eros* in a marriage would put an unnecessary stress on the relationship.

However, in previous centuries this was not so. Romance is still considered unnecessary in many contemporary Eastern and traditional cultures, where parents usually arrange their children's marriages. Marriages were arranged in biblical times also, which accounts for the absence of direct teaching on dating in the Bible. Our modern Western view that romantic love is the main foundation for marriage probably dates back to the Renaissance, the French romance courts of the 1700s, and the body of popular literature extolling romance that grew out of the Enlightenment period.

The older method of parentally arranged marriages had its own problems. Women were often denied any choice in the matter. On the other hand, we might doubt whether they suffered any more under that system when it was applied by godly, caring parents than they do today with the "taste-test" method and its fifty-percent divorce rate.

Going back to arranging marriages is neither possible nor desirable in our society. But romantic love is not a sufficient condition for marriage either. Romantic desires should be subjected to far more foundational and enduring criteria. The greatest of these is Christian love.

Some who are already married feel helpless because they cannot sense the romantic love they used to feel. They should find hope in knowing they don't need a new injection of *eros* to improve their marriages. Instead, they need to develop the ability to love deeply and biblically. As they cultivate this ability, even the romantic dimension of their relationship will likely blossom. This romantic love will be different but more satisfying than what they lost. No wonder those who have a committed marriage relationship report the highest level of sexual satisfaction! According to a new sex survey done by the University of Chicago (as reported in the cover story of *Time*, October 17, 1994), "Married couples have the most sex and are the most likely to have orgasms when they do." This and other recent studies only confirm what the Bible has always taught.

Developing Christian Love

Eros can easily be confused with Christian love. In both, we may be willing to give unselfishly. In both, the level of communication may seem quite intimate. The key difference is that our giving and communication in romantic relationships is motivated by the good feelings and excitement we constantly derive from the relationship. If these feelings disappear, the basis for giving also disappears.

> *Eros* can easily be confused with Christian love.

Stated differently, with *eros*, when we no longer receive good feelings, we no longer feel able to give as before. We begin to focus on the fact that we are not experiencing love feelings anymore. Although we may explain our problems in terms of behavior rather than love feelings ("She just nags and overeats these days"), we are actually expressing the absence of present love feelings. Married people often complain that their spouses no longer communicate or be-

33

have like they did when dating. But this change, whether real or perceived, is not the issue. The real issue is that we no longer feel the surge of *eros* feelings like we used to. We can be sure our spouse had problems when we were dating, but they either went unnoticed or seemed unimportant in light of overwhelming *eros* desire. Later, without constant *eros* stimulation, we begin to notice the irritating aspects of our spouse's behavior. The faults we were willing to overlook before seem to have become worse. We may experience pitiful suffering and confusion as we wonder what went wrong.

Here is an exciting truth: The Bible teaches that practicing Christian love is a *learned* ability. Therefore, Christians need never be the victim of a capricious "love" that comes and goes. According to 1 John 4:7, no one practices Christian love naturally apart from God's power. The New Testament also teaches that a Christian who consistently practices Christian love is living at the highest level of spiritual maturity. (See Romans 13:10; John 13:34; 15:12; 2 Peter 1:5–8; and 1 John 2:10.) Ideally, we should develop the ability to love in this way *before* we attempt marriage. In cases where this has not occurred, couples must learn Christian love under the sometimes severe pressure of marriage itself—a project that may be uncomfortable but is definitely possible.

> Practicing Christian love is a *learned* ability.

Christian love can be expressed at various levels of friendship, whether casual or intimate. But in marriage we hope to be able to love at the deepest, or most intimate, level. The closer the relationship, the more demanding sacrificial loving becomes. We find it relatively easy to protect ourselves from an uncomfortable level of sacrifice in more distant friendships. At most, we may have to give for a limited period of time, but we can always withdraw afterward. But in marriage, we are usually together on a daily basis in the most trying circumstances. There is little room for retreat.

No wonder many newly married people find themselves

34

confused: Why were they able to get along with their spouses before marriage but not after marriage? The answer often is the lack of real intimacy in the previous relationships compared to that required in marriage. Real closeness and commitment will test the love-giving capability of both partners.

How Will I Know?

Popular singer Whitney Houston poses the question, "How will I know if he really loves me?" The Bible can't answer a question like this because it relates to the *eros* myth. A more important question is:

**How can we know before marrying
that we have the ability to practice Christian love
at the most intimate level?**

The only way to know for sure is to ascertain that we already practice Christian love in *non-romantic* intimate relationships. In such friendships, there will not be any chance of confusing Christian love with erotic love. If we succeed in building intimate non-romantic relationships outside marriage, we will almost certainly be able to practice Christian love in marriage even when the *eros* feelings subside.

If you are already married, probably no one needs to convince you of the importance of learning a deeper form of love-giving. On the other hand, those who feel fatalistic despair need to submit to the truth of God's Word. God can and will teach us what we need to know in the area of self-giving love. If you are in a distressed marriage, you should realize that the pain you are feeling is the pressure God wants to use to lift you up to a higher level of Christian maturity. (See 1 Corinthians 10:13 and James 1:4.) As a married person, you also can learn how to practice mature Christian love in other relationships outside marriage. These other relationships usually have less tension and lower expectations initially. The skills you develop in non-erotic relationships can, as a rule, be successfully applied to your marriage relationship as well.

The Key to Successful Marriage

The key to marital success is not finding the right person. Neither is it discovering true love. If you want to understand God's pattern for success in marriage, you will discover that

The key is not to *find* the right person, but to *become* the right person: a person who has learned to practice Christian love at the most intimate level.

With this premise in mind, we now turn to an in-depth definition of Christian love, along with considerations about how to grow in love in various levels of relationship. By studying the next two chapters, it should be possible to determine where you stand in your ability to practice Christian love. Then you can identify your weaknesses and begin to draw on the power of God to help you change in specific areas. Eventually, you will learn to practice Christian love in the most difficult but rewarding of all relationships: the intimate relationship. This is the level you must master if you seek a successful marriage.

Before you can turn to God for help in becoming the kind of person who will succeed in marriage, you must surrender your life to Jesus Christ. Christ will change your life in the most profound way, but only if you are willing to give him the keys and let him drive your life. Listen to his words: "He who believes in Me . . . 'From his innermost being shall flow rivers of living waters'. . . . this He spoke of the Spirit . . ." (John 7:38).

This is not a superficial change. Jesus offers you a complete overhaul of your innermost self. He will forgive your sins, placing them on his own Cross, and begin a transforming personal relationship with you today if you will turn to him and ask for it. Then it will become possible for your thoughts, feelings, and actions to change permanently. As God says through the apostle Paul, ". . . do not be conformed to this world, but be transformed by the renewing of your mind . . ." (Romans 12:2).

If you are not certain you have ever initiated this personal relationship with God, you should do so now. Just turn to him in your heart and acknowledge that you are guilty of sins, that you need God's forgiveness. Put your trust in Jesus Christ as the one whose death can forgive your sin and open the way to a personal relationship with God.

Notes

1. The word *agapao* is not always used in a technical sense in the New Testament. However, most authors do use it to refer to Christian love, or to the love of God, even though they may also use other words (such as *phileo*) to refer to Christian love as well. Therefore, even though there are exceptions, we can speak in terms of the general usage of the word in the New Testament. In this book, we will use the term Christian love instead of *agape*. For further commentary on the question of words for love in the New Testament, see Anders Nygren, *Agape and Eros* (Philadelphia: Westminster Press, 1953), or Earl F. Palmer, *Love Has Its Reasons* (Waco, Tex.: Word Books, 1977).
2. Pure Prairie League, "Falling In and Out of Love," from *Bustin' Out*, RCA, 4656.
3. Palmer, pp. 38–40.
4. "The Role of Cohabitation in Declining Rates of Marriage," *Journal of Marriage and the Family*, Vol. 53 (1991), pp. 913–927. Children of divorced parents also tend to cohabit more than children of intact families. This indicates again the snowballing effect of marital failure in America. "Influence of the Marital History of Parents on the Marital and Cohabitational Experiences of Children," *American Journal of Sociology*, Vol. 96 (1991), pp. 88–894.
5. In a nationwide study completed at the University of Wisconsin in 1992, based on 13,000 adults, the researchers found that couples who cohabited before marriage "reported greater marital conflict and poorer communication" in marriage, were "less committed to the institution of marriage," and "perceived greater likelihood of divorce." They also found that "longer cohabitation was associated with higher likelihood of divorce." The cohabited couples reported that they experienced "lower quality marriages." Thompson & Colella, "Cohabitation and Marital Stability: Quality or Commitment," *Journal of Marriage and Family*, Vol. 54 (1992), pp. 259–267.

THREE

WHAT DOES CHRISTIAN INTIMACY LOOK LIKE?

True friendship is a plant of slow growth, and must undergo and withstand the shocks of adversity before it is entitled to the appellation.

—GEORGE WASHINGTON

To love as Christ loves is to let our love be a practical and not a sentimental thing.

—SIR CHARLES VILLIERS STANFORD

When you think about your regular friends, you may conclude, like many, that while your friendships are valuable and you really enjoy them, they are not necessarily all that deep, or intimate. Barry had lots of friends and often referred to people as his "best friend." Yet, when he got married, Barry's wife complained that he seemed to be avoiding intimacy. He couldn't understand her problem and pointed out that his buddies never offered this sort of complaint. "The way I relate is good enough for them. Why isn't it good enough for you?" he challenged.

After agreeing to do a study of his relational life, Barry learned his friendships outside his marriage were not as deep as he thought. The elements missing in those relationships were exactly the same things his new wife longed for in their marriage. He realized that the level of intimacy in his other friendships was inadequate for a marriage. As a gift to his wife, he needed to take his relational ability up another notch and fill in the blanks in his capability.

How can we know if we are accepting a standard of relational closeness that will fail us in marriage? How can we know if we have blind spots in the way we relate to others? The first solution to this question is knowing in principle what intimacy looks like. Most of us have ideas of what intimacy is, often based on experiences in our families. Some of us frankly admit we have no clear idea what intimacy is, and we are mainly guessing. Let's look at a model of friendship based on principles in Scripture to see whether our conceptions of relational closeness go far enough.

How to Recognize Intimacy

Personal relationships vary in depth and quality. For the purpose of discussion, we will describe three general levels of friendship: casual, close, and intimate. With each level of friendship we will also discuss three areas of sharing, each of which is present in proper measure in a healthy relationship. These areas are common experience, personal inner working, and emotional sharing. Before going on, let's consider definitions for each of these areas of sharing. The next page compares these levels of relationship in chart form.

- *Common Experience*: To share common experience means we spend time and do things with those we love. By sharing experiences together, we develop a base of shared memories and feelings that become part of our relationship. While Christian love can be practiced in new relationships (Jesus clearly did this), deeper Christian love relationships will require more common experience.
- *Personal Inner Working*: To share our personal inner working with another means we choose to reveal what's inside: our hopes, fears, dreams, struggles, and other personal matters. Personal inner working also refers to our accumulating

40

knowledge of the other person's internal makeup. This kind of sharing is communication. We can measure the communication in a relationship by how much we are learning and disclosing about what makes us tick on the inside. This understanding should go both directions in a healthy relationship.

Levels of Relationships

	Common Experience	Personal Inner Working	Emotional Sharing
Casual	*Sporadic* contact. Tends to be short-term and somewhat superficial.	*General* searching into the other's interests, goals, likes and dislikes, background, spiritual experiences, priorities, problems, and frustrations.	Visible interest, warmth, enthusiasm. "Politeness" means negative feelings are only shared if necessary, and then carefully.
Close	*Regular* time spent. Feel the need to keep up time spent. Quality time included. Shared goals and interests.	Freedom to ask pointed, personal questions about other relationships, feelings, etc. Beginning to understand each other's deeper problems and potentials. Able to promote others' potential and help with problems.	Loyalty, affection, and gratitude. More honest about disappointments, but also careful to encourage.
Intimate	*Extensive* time commitment. Availability has few limits. Shared worlds, including shared goals, activities, and other people. Significant backlog of common experience.	Completely open communication. Common commitment to develop each other's character. Affirmation and confrontation occurs both ways. Accountability.	Expressing the same feelings as under "close," but with even more freedom to share openly. Emotional giving is constructive and controlled. Commitment to share positive or nurturing feelings for the sake of the other, even when not spontaneous.

- *Emotional Sharing*: Emotional communication means we share our feelings and understand one another's feelings. Because we are created with emotions, an unemotional relationship is incomplete. In each level of relationship we should not only feel emotion, but effectively communicate our feelings, especially those feelings that will edify or nurture our loved one. For instance, we may think we have communicated affection, but if the other person has not sensed the affection, our communication has been ineffective.

The Casual Relationship

Now let's consider the chart, reading each row from left to right.

Common Experience	Personal Inner Working	Emotional Sharing
Sporadic contact. Tends to be short-term and somewhat superficial.	*General* searching into the other's interests, goals, likes and dislikes, background, spiritual experiences, priorities, problems, and frustrations.	Visible interest, warmth, enthusiasm. "Politeness" means negative feelings are only shared if necessary, and then carefully.

Common Experience

The term "sporadic contact" in the chart means that personal contact in this kind of relationship is usually not deliberate. There may be periodic contact as we run into each other, but there is no planned effort to get together regularly. If we happen to experience no contact with each other at all for a period of time, we feel no uneasiness. Neighbors, fellow employees, casual dates, and people in our church all have the potential to become enjoyable casual friends.

We don't use the word "superficial" here negatively. It only means that we don't usually discuss deep personal matters. Most of our friendships probably fit this description, which is normal. But if we discover that *all* of our relationships are superficial, we have a problem. We will discuss how to address this problem in Chapter 4.

Personal Inner Working

In this column, the chart says, "General searching into their interests, goals, likes and dislikes, background, spiritual experiences, priorities, problems, and frustrations." We search for understanding in these areas by asking appropriate questions. When we discover one thing, we naturally follow up our initial question with another and another until we understand that area.

> Some people are so relationally passive that they don't know how to explore the inner workings of another person.

Some people are so relationally passive that they don't know how to explore the inner workings of another person. Such people may be considered "shy" because they feel they don't know what to say when talking to a new person. In established relationships, including marriage, the passive relater usually depends on the other person to sense his or her problems or feelings and act accordingly. But we will not be effective either in "drawing out" or understanding others unless we cultivate the ability to ask questions while truly listening to the answers. Taking interest in another is a learned skill requiring initiative and practice. The same is true of learning to share our own feelings.

The real problem with shy people is usually a form of self-centered passivity. Self-centeredness in this context means that we tend to think about ourselves rather than about others. Our fears and insecurities often inhibit us from "getting outside ourselves" and into others. Although shy people may be able to focus attention on another person for short periods of time, such sporadic interest may be insufficient to really understand the other person well.

This ability to take interest in others and actively explore their personal inner working requires *initiative in relating.* This means that we are not dependent on others to tell us about themselves. We have learned how to initiate and stimulate communication, by taking our attention off ourselves, then patiently and sensitively questioning others and listening to their answers. Even in existing relationships, we will often find that this is difficult unless we practice it regularly. Fortunately, initiative is a learned relational skill. We can develop it if we lack it, and God can also help us correct this deficiency. In the next chapter we will discuss practical ways to work through our shortcomings in this area. We are not fated to live a defeated life, especially when it comes to our relationships.

People can express self-centeredness in different ways. For instance, an extrovert may hope to convince others he is worthy of attention. He should instead learn to give others *his* attention. Both tendencies, shyness and boastfulness, inhibit people from giving their full attention to others.

The Careful Listener

Both shy people and extroverts need to draw more sense of identity, humility, and courage from their standing with God. Only then can they develop the listening skills they need for deep relationships. James urges, ". . . let everyone be quick to hear, slow to speak . . ." (James 1:19).

Careless listeners are often preoccupied, perhaps thinking of the next question, or how their last comment was perceived. The result is usually a short answer from those with whom they are conversing, and more uneasiness as they wonder what to say next. Fruitful and enjoyable conversations usually only develop when both people sense a genuine interest in each other. We can cultivate this interest in others as we discover new and exciting things about them. This is at the heart of what it means to become a good listener.

To learn about another's personal inner working, we need to ask questions. But we should include some open questions—those that cannot be answered by a yes or no. For instance, the question, "Do you like your school?" is a closed question. We may very well hear an answer such as "Yeah, it's cool." Now what do we do? We could follow with an open question: "Really. What's so cool about it?" Or we could have asked in the first place, "How do you feel about your school?" In either event, we would more likely hear an answer that includes some commentary and more interesting content, including information about the person, not just the school. By expressing opinions, people reveal something about themselves.

As careful listeners, we soon discover that the answer to one question naturally raises several other questions. Very quickly, others realize they are talking to a good listener and become interested in talking much more freely. Remember, we should be looking into others' interests, not waiting to tell them about our own. They will probably become interested in our life as the relationship develops. But this is not the goal—the goal is to genuinely show love to others by seeking to learn more about them.

Emotional Sharing

When trying to get to know others, nothing helps more than an authentic display of interest. So often our questions are rhetorical; we don't really care what the answer is. But when we ask questions, digest the answers, and then ask more questions while visually displaying interest and understanding (through appropriate eye contact, smiles, posture, and gestures), we will find that most people enjoy talking about themselves, leading to healthy casual relationships.

Warmth and enthusiasm are also important. Most of us have met people who are very warm, and we have felt an immediate attraction to them. But talking to someone who seems uninterested or unmoved by our words is depressing and annoying. Some of us may need to carefully observe warm and enthusiastic people to discover how their body language and demeanor communicate their interest. By practicing this kind of emotional communication, we will find scores of open doors for rewarding casual friendships. These relationships, in turn, can often develop into deeper friendships.

This insight also applies to those who are involved in relationships that seem to have "lost all the fizz," including marriage. For instance, when we have difficulty beginning positive conversations, many of us develop the bad habit of "jabbing" the other person verbally in order to get some kind of response. This practice could be called "pigtail pulling." Pigtail pulling derives its name from a typical practice of ten-year-old boys. A boy at this age may feel attracted to a girl in his class but lacks the maturity to express his feelings in a positive way. Instead, he pulls her pigtail (or kicks her in the shin) during recess. She yells at him and perhaps chases him, thus completing an immature relational interaction which, although not ideal in the mind of the boy, is better than nothing.

Teenage boys are especially prone to pigtail pulling. "Hey, if you need help lifting that, just give me a whimper," jeers one good-natured high-schooler as he throws an elbow at his buddy. Boys often view this kind of banter as fun and even intimate, and in proper measure, such jabs have their place in healthy relationships. But there's a problem. These boys may know no other way to interact emotionally. They like each other, and want to say something that engages, but the only thing that comes to mind is a joking put-down.

In the same way, a husband may come home and give his wife a pinch on the rear with the comment, "You're putting on a little beef!" He may not seriously object to her figure; he just wants to have some fun and "relate." Why is she so oversensitive? To the immature pigtail-puller, everyone is being weird and thin-skinned when they can't see the fun in his comments. The results of such immature approaches, however, are usually disappointing.

If you are struggling with this kind of defeat, try stepping out and initiating some conversations, either with your spouse or other friends. Specifically, try to explore the other person's interests and respond with warmth and enthusiasm. Resist the impulse to give advice or to begin sharing about yourself unless the other person directly asks. You may be surprised by how quickly you experience positive results. Most people are thirsty for a relationship with someone who knows how to take a sincere interest in them and will usually respond eagerly when the opportunity arises.

The Close Relationship

Common Experience	Personal Inner Working	Emotional Sharing
Regular time spent. Feel the need to maintain time spent. Quality time included. Shared goals and interests.	Freedom to ask pointed, personal questions about other relationships, feelings, etc. Beginning to understand each other's deeper problems and potentials. Able to promote others' potential and help with problems.	Loyalty, affection, and gratitude. More honest about disappointments, but also careful to encourage.

Common Experience

In a close relationship, we will naturally find that sharing is deeper, more frequent, and more constant in every area. The description of a close relationship above says "Regular time spent." This means we normally spend time with a close friend at least once or twice a week, in addition to group situations. Less time investment than this would make it difficult to build a close relationship. Involvement in the same ministry or home fellowship group provides a natural and healthy context for building closer friendships.

A relationship is close when it has become a priority. Therefore, we do not *hope* for enough time for the relationship, we *make* time for it. The phrase "feel the need to maintain time spent" means that if we have not had contact with a close friend for more than a few days, we feel the absence and naturally want to reestablish contact as soon as possible. The phrase "quality time included" doesn't mean all our time is spent in serious or personal discussion. In fact, this is not desirable because it would be unnatural. However, it does mean we frequently initiate quality discussions.

When the chart says "shared interests," it means that with close friends we have made an effort to join into their interests. It should not be necessary for the other person to already have many interests in common with our own, although this certainly makes things easier. Our friends may become involved in our interests eventually, but according to the idea of self-giving Christian love, we should be willing to initiate giving by seeking involvement in our friends' interests.

The same principle applies to time. Time is perhaps our most precious commodity. Often we are willing to give other things—such as money or possessions—but not our time. We often expect others to arrange their schedules around ours. This sometimes amounts to a conditional relationship: We will spend time together only if it is convenient in our existing schedule. We should not feel obligated to participate in *all* of our friends' interests, but we should be able to point to some cases where we have come out of our own comfort zone to spend time in activity with our friends.

Extending ourselves in order to develop common experience is a basic area of giving in relationships, including marriage. When couples are unwilling to negotiate common areas in their schedules and interests, a serious barrier to intimacy results. Couples defy the obvious when they expect closeness, even though their schedules provide little common experience. Someone has to initiate giving in this area, and normally the husband should be the leader. (We will discuss the topic of "headship" in Chapter 9. In Ephesians 5:25 and parallel Scriptures, husbands are urged to *initiate* self-sacrifice.) Creative alternatives may also offer promise to both partners. Certainly, we can always take turns. However, we will never avoid the necessity to deny self and give sacrificially if we expect to practice Christian love. That means saying no to my interests at times for the sake of being with the one I love.

Personal Inner Working

The closer our relationships grow, the greater our freedom to explore our friends' inner workings. As we explore, we will begin to form impressions of their strengths and weaknesses. With this personal knowledge comes the responsibility to encourage the potential good and, at times, to point out areas of weakness.

We need to understand our friends' other important relationships, such as dating relationships, family, and other friends. With close friends, we should also be exploring and understanding their spiritual lives. In addition to practicing the same careful listening that began at the casual level, we need to model openness by being open about ourselves.

As our understanding grows, we should also spend time thinking and praying about our friends when we are not together. This discipline is an important element in mature love giving. Our input will tend to be haphazard and off target if we think about others only when present with them. Just as we can tell when a friend has spent time thinking about something we shared, we can also tell when he hasn't given it a second thought. Likewise, our friends can tell whether we are thinking about them when they are not with us. When we regularly and sacrificially think and pray about others when not with them, God will give us insight we can use to help. As a result, they will tend to feel appreciation and will assign more credibility to our views.

In close relationships, we should allow the other person to

discover our inner life as well. We should cultivate the ability to respond honestly to their probing, disclosing what we are thinking and feeling about matters in our own life. For many of us, this may be a scary exercise because we have learned to derive a sense of safety from hiding our inner life. But while vulnerability with others is risky, it is necessary if we want the security that comes from knowing that someone knows us deeply and still loves us. As Christians we have an advantage in cultivating this kind of vulnerability because we know that God knows everything about us and still accepts us. Therefore, we can afford to risk self-disclosure with others.

Emotional Sharing

Underestimating the role of emotions in relationships is a big mistake. For a relationship to grow close, we must effectively communicate. "Loyalty" is mentioned on the chart. Loyalty is the emotional expression of commitment. Commitment means we communicate by word and action our willingness to stand by our friends, even in difficult situations.

Also mentioned is "affection." Some of us find it difficult to communicate affection. Those of us who have such inhibitions may have to actually plan out statements to say when we are with a loved one. If we have not developed the habit of expressing affection, we may never express it spontaneously. We might not like planning out statements ahead of time, even though they are true. But why should we feel uneasy about planning out things to say, when we never feel awkward about planning out recreational activities?

The apostle Paul suggests this in Ephesians 4:29: "Let no unwholesome word proceed from your mouth, but only such a word as is good for edification . . . that it may give grace to those who hear." Hebrews 10:24–25 says we should "*consider* how to stimulate one another . . . encouraging one another" (emphasis added). Both of these verses, and others as well, suggest that we need to *think ahead* about our communication to people. As we practice this kind of communication, it will gradually become more natural.

The chart mentions sharing our feelings of gratitude. We should be grateful not simply for immediate favors others have done for us ("Thanks for the dinner"), but more importantly, we should express gratitude for the relationship itself ("I really appreciate our friendship because . . ."). These are the kinds of moments that bind people together in Christian love. Vulnerable emotional statements constitute a very real type of giving, often meeting our loved one's most basic needs. As such, they are indispensable to Christian love.

The Intimate Relationship

Common Experience	Personal Inner Working	Emotional Sharing
Extensive time commitment. Availability has few limits. Shared worlds, including shared goals, activities, and other people. Significant backlog of common experience.	Completely open communication. Common commitment to develop each other's character. Affirmation and confrontation occurs both ways. Accountability.	Expressing the same feelings as under "close," but with even more freedom to share openly. Emotional giving is constructive and controlled. Commitment to share positive or nurturing feelings for the sake of the other, even when not spontaneous.

Common Experience

When the chart says *"extensive* time commitment," it means that intimate friends naturally spend large amounts of time together. Merely spending a lot of time together will not guarantee intimate friendship. But no one can build ongoing intimacy without spending time. Spouses, engaged couples, and best friends should be our intimate relationships.

The phrase "significant backlog of common experience" means the relationship has gone on long enough to build up a history together. This sense of continuity and the knowledge of each other's reliability usually lead to basic trust, which in turn enables candid communication. If we have only recently started spending time with someone, we lack a realistic basis for this level of intimacy. Notions of instant intimacy in relationships are usually referring to erotic types of love rather than an investment type of love.

The phrase "shared worlds, including shared goals, activities, and other people" means that we understand much of what goes on in the other person's life—in part because many of the same things are now also a part of our own life. For instance, we have made an effort to know to some extent the important people in our friends' lives.

At the intimate level, we may notice new problems in our relationships. At lower levels of friendship, we might have experienced harmony because our expectations of the relationship were lower, making us easier to please. At deeper levels, however, some of us will become very difficult to please because a whole new set of expectations applies. This leads to relational demands, and the belief that such demands are fair. If our expectations are disappointed, we wrongly tend to seek ways of forcing compliance to our demands. This will result in resistance from our friends and frustration on our part. Listen to these two quotes from young women on a major Christian college campus:

> The ability to make another person feel loved and valuable is what I look for in a guy. I'm not married, but I've seen the verse in the Bible where husbands are told to love their wives. I think this includes making a woman feel worthwhile and secure.

> The most important quality I look for in a guy is his ability to love unconditionally. I know that I am far from perfect, but in a world like ours today where husbands and

wives divorce over the smallest differences, it is important that he be able to love me, even with all my faults.

Don't these thoughts sound familiar? Both contain an element of truth, but there's a problem. In both these views we see the belief that success in marriage is based on finding someone who will give the right kind of love to *me*. Neither acknowledge the far more important issue—am I able to give mature love to *others*? One openly acknowledges her hope that a man will make her "feel worthwhile and secure." But if we plan to draw our worth and security from another human being, we are headed for trouble, and frankly, we are not ready for success in marriage.

Maturing Christians learn that no human, including even our most intimate friends, will ever meet all or even most of our expectations or emotional needs. Instead of coercing others to love us the way we want to be loved (or to "just do their part" as we would probably say), God eventually teaches us to drop these love demands. This decision is an expression of our trust that God will meet all of our needs in his own way and timing. We learn to draw our worth and security directly from our identity in Christ. (For an in-depth discussion of this crucial point, see Dennis McCallum, *Walking in Victory: Experiencing the Power of Your Identity in Christ* [Colorado Springs: Navpress, 1994].) Only on this basis can we focus on how we can give to our loved ones rather than on how they should be giving to us.

To understand this distinction, consider the difference between possessiveness and availability. Demanding time from our friends is usually motivated by considerations of self-advantage. Such demands are therefore foreign to the idea of sacrificial Christian love. Instead, *both* people should agree on the amount of time necessary to maintain the relationship. If we need to criticize our friends for lack of availability, such criticism should be for their benefit—to assist them in overcoming irresponsible tendencies when relating. Even though we may also benefit as a result of our criticism because our friends change their behavior, we are acting sacrificially if our motives are pure. We can usually tell rather easily whether people are criticizing us for their own advantage or for ours.

Personal Inner Working

With intimate friends we share all but that which would be selfish and unedifying. In other words, we are willing to explain any aspect of our past or our makeup without feeling the need for secrecy. Openness is an important feature of intimacy, because many people have problems they never tell anyone about. Unfortunately, unless we have someone with whom we intimately communicate, we will always feel a sense of loneliness. When we fail to open up about our life we can say with some truth, "No one understands." But this is actually a confession that we have been ineffective in building the type of relationship where we could expect understanding.

At the same time, we should not feel free to blurt out feelings that are wounding, offensive, or threatening to an intimate friend, as we shall see later.

The word "commitment" appears often in the intimate column of our table. Commitment is a crucial element in intimacy, and this accounts for much of the failure in modern relationships. In our culture today, many fear commitment to another. Growing Christians, on the other hand, realize that we fear commitment mainly because we worry that it will interfere with our determination to live selfish lives. This would be a legitimate fear, unless we have already waived all right to a self-centered lifestyle. To the Christian who has received freely of the grace of Christ, self-sacrificing love should be less threatening, even at a committed level.

Our growing understanding of intimate friends leads to the moral obligation to use that knowledge for their good. We become committed to their character development. Such commitment sometimes involves confrontation in love. The ability to caringly and effectively confront another is one of the most difficult relational skills involved in mature love relationships. It is also one of the most selfless.

In the non-Christian world, love relationships are expected to make us feel good. Therefore the secular concept of love tends to be either domination or permissiveness, depending on what people believe will lead to the best results for self. They have no clear basis for always doing what is best for the other person as in Christian love, because doing what is best for others may result in painful feelings and experiences for "me." When confrontation does occur in secular relationships, it is usually out of anger or personal hurt. But indulging personal feelings of hurt or anger has nothing to do with acting for the benefit of others. When you step on your dog's tail, he may turn around and bite. But when he does so, he is not acting out of a concern for your well-being.

Christian love is not this way. As already discussed, we should learn to confront for the good of others, not because their problems are irritating us, even though we may be feeling irritation as well. What are the elements of loving confrontation?

> The secular concept of love tends to be either domination or permissiveness, depending on what people believe will lead to the best results for self.

- First, we have to spend sufficient time reflecting on our loved one's life to determine the underlying causes of their problems. Prayer, reading, and consultation with mature Christians can help us understand why people would have the sort of problems we are encountering. If we realize the problem was mainly an isolated incident, or an area of which our loved one was already aware, we should consider simply dropping it (Proverbs 19:11). If, on the other hand, we realize the problem is part of a pattern the other person needs to deal with, dropping it would *not* be the loving thing to do (1 Thessalonians 5:14).

- Next, we need to plan how we will approach the problem with our loved one. What sort of approach will be disarming? How will we express our positive feelings and commitment to him or her? When would be a good time to bring it up?
- Finally, what will we say? How should we express the problem without becoming inflammatory? Considering how difficult it is for people to hear criticism, how will we make it easier? Is there any way in which we see the same or similar problem in our own life? What will we suggest should be done to see improvement in the area?

For some, confrontation comes easier than affirmation. Have we learned the power of gracious compliments and encouragement? For most of us, these are skills that come only with practice. If our friends complain that we are not very encouraging, or that we are overly critical, it may become necessary to plan encouragement out. Such planning should take place when we are not actually with them. During our time of prayer and reflection, God will often remind us of something we appreciate about them, or about something good they did. If we are not easily satisfied with others' actions (i.e., we are perfectionists), we may have to deliberately reevaluate our view of things, rejecting our own hyper-negativity. In this way we can actually cultivate appreciation of others. Did our loved one do something that could have been better but definitely had an element of good—at least in intention? If so, we should determine to speak about it in clear terms.

If we are not very effusive and warm in our speech, we will need to think about how to word our encouragement in a way that is not awkward or cold. We should reject unlikely fears such as, "She may get a big head." It is much more likely that she may not even realize we complimented her! Egotism is rarely the result of being complimented or appreciated. It more often results from insecurity in the relationship than from verbal affirmation.

Our table says confrontation and affirmation should go *both* ways in an intimate relationship. If confrontation goes only one way (which very often happens), it betrays an unnatural hierarchy in the relationship. If others are too passive and will not confront us, perhaps we should ask them to! Is it possible that the other person will not confront us because we are not receptive to criticism? Constructive criticism is an act of vulnerability and love, and we should express gratitude for it. This kind of commitment is "accountability." One of the things that may cause us to avoid intimate relationships is our fear of accountability. We will see later that this kind of autonomous attitude is extremely harmful in a marriage relationship.

We should also be accountable to one another for how we will respond when communication breaks down in the relationship. This happens at times even in the best of relationships. The important thing is how we respond during such times. In healthy intimate relationships, both parties know their own sinful tendencies in this area, and they agree to respond to reminders to avoid these tendencies. Some of us are inclined to lash out with hurtful words, while others withdraw in sulky silence. Still others ignore the conflict and act as though nothing is wrong. Have we identified our own tendencies in this area and acknowledged them to our intimate friends? Have we given them the "green light" to call on us to desist from self-protective and punishing responses during conflict?

Emotional Sharing

The same emotions expressed in the close relationship should be expressed at the intimate level. Here they are even more appropriate. At this level, many of us are tempted to think that expressing our nurturing emotions is unnecessary. After all, we expressed love feelings before, so why can't we assume that our loved one remembers? Why do we have to say it again? The reason, of course, is that people need to hear often that we love and appreciate them. Expressing caring feelings never becomes unnecessary, no matter how many times we have expressed them before. Our goal should be to help the other person feel consistently loved. Effective emotional communication is an art to be highly prized.

What about our negative feelings? The closer a relationship, the more negative feelings we will encounter. Are we free to lash out in hurt and anger? Are we being dishonest if we feel jealous, angry, or disinterested and fail to say so?

The Bible says we should *not* feel free to blurt out feelings in words that are wounding, offensive, or threatening. (See Ephesians 4:29.) The term "unwholesome word" in this passage does not primarily mean a word that is profane or dirty. It means words that rot or despoil others. The passage is telling us not to speak in a way that is destructive of others. Those who say they hate their friends, or spouses who say they wish they were divorced from their mates, are indulging in an ungodly form of fleshliness. Such feelings should be shared with a helpful third party, such as a counselor or mature Christian friend, in a setting that will not wound our loved one.

Instead of blurting, we should realize the need to gain emotional control of our own negative or demanding impulses before speaking. This is what James means when he refers to "controlling the tongue" (James 3:1ff). Spiritual maturity will lead us to go first to God and ask where we might be in the wrong, or, if we are not wrong, how we can communicate effectively and graciously. Many plead at this point that to withhold harmful comments and punishing behavior would be "dishonest" and would constitute repressing one's feelings. However, neither of these complaints is valid biblically.

In the first place, as Christians, we should be concerned with what is true, not just what we feel. Scripture is clear on this point: Our feelings are not always reliable guides to reality. (See 2 Corinthians 5:7; 1 John 3:20; Proverbs 3:5; and Genesis 4:6–7.) For instance, suppose I feel hurt, abandoned, and jealous when my spouse decides to do something with someone else on a given evening. Yet, upon further reflection, God may show me that we have spent a good amount of time together lately, and that my spouse's other activity is important. This last realization was not reflected in my feelings initially. In this case, holding back my initial negative reactions and allowing the Holy Spirit to enlighten me would be an important part of my role as a mature partner.

When we restrain our impulses long enough to hear God, he may show us our own part in a conflict. He may show us other aspects of the situation that didn't occur to us at first. Or he may simply show us the way of humility, grace, and forgiveness in that situation. We are not *repressing* our feelings in an unhealthy way; we are merely *controlling* our responses with God's help. This kind of self-control is a fruit of the Holy Spirit (Galatians 5:23). "Outbursts of anger," on the other hand, are of the flesh, as are jealousies and dissensions (Galatians 5:19–21).

Marriage therapists observe that couples tend to reward or to punish each other in approximately the same measure. This tendency is called *reciprocity*. However, counselors point out that they do *not* see reciprocating punishing behavior between happily married couples. This is an important observation, backed up by abundant research.[1] Some authorities speculate that happy couples feel no need to reciprocate punishment because their overall expectations of rewarding feelings from the relationship allow them to overlook isolated punishing behavior. This is certainly probable. However, the Christian theorist would also argue that happy couples may be exercising their free will in deciding to deny selfish impulses, forbear, and forgive in a conflict situation. Christians would further argue that such forbearance is a major *cause* of happiness in marriage, not just the result. Of course, any quality pushed to an extreme could distort a relationship. Forbearance is not always the answer, but for most of us, it should be the answer far more often than we think.

Notes

1. Neil S. Jacobson and Gayla Margolin, *Marital Therapy: Strategies Based on Social Learning and Behavior Exchange Principles* (New York: Bruner/Mazel, 1979), pp. 14–16. The behaviorist model sees all behavior as the result of stimuli, usually from the other partner in the marriage. Thus, "... the members of a marital relationship are constantly influencing and controlling one another, so that it is arbitrary and downright misleading to ... assign singular causal importance to one person's behavior" (p. 14). This is usually true, but can be changed at any time that the individual (especially a Christian) elects to break the cycle of negativity and initiate love giving out of self-sacrifice. Naturally, secular counselors such as these cannot call on their clients for any truly sacrificial behavior.

FOUR
LEARNING CHRISTIAN LOVE

Maturity begins to grow when you can sense your concern for others outweighing your concern for yourself.

—JOHN MACNAUGHTON

Having studied various levels of love relationships, we are now able to better assess our present ability to build Christian love relationships. Nothing will be more important in forming a successful marriage than a proven ability to relate in a biblical way, even at the deepest level. By comparing the chart in Chapter 3 with our present relationships, we can develop a personal love inventory. Then it should be easier to see where we need development in the future.

Personal Love Inventory

On a piece of paper, write a list of your friends and compare the areas of sharing in each type of relationship with the descriptions given in Chapter 3. Here is an example:

John:
    Common Experience: Sporadic contact. We sometimes have meaningful talk, but usually not.
    Personal Inner Working: We discuss some personal areas, but I don't feel the freedom to ask him about all areas of his life. Sometimes I sense he's holding back.
    Emotional: Not much overt emotion is expressed toward

each other. We only express emotion when we watch football.

This description, when compared with the chart, indicates the relationship with John is a casual one. Naturally, most of our relationships will be casual. This is not bad. However, if *all* of our relationships are casual, we have reason to question our ability to build an intimate relationship in marriage. Again, why do married couples report that they never had problems relating to their friends before marriage but suddenly have problems with their spouses once married? The likely reason is that intimacy tests our relational skills more than surface relationships ever do. Relational problems that may go unnoticed in our single lives cannot hide in the face of marital intimacy.

This is the best reason for seeking out and developing intimate relationships before marriage, especially in non-romantic friendships. If we are not successfully loving people at the intimate level before marriage, what makes us think we will be able to do so after marriage? Likewise, if we are married, but have no intimate relationships outside our marriage, perhaps the problem is not with our spouse after all!

> If we are not successfully loving people at the intimate level before marriage, what makes us think we will be able to do so after marriage?

Experience shows that unless we have successfully built at least one non-romantic intimate Christian love relationship, doing so within marriage will be extraordinarily difficult, notwithstanding our present sense of closeness with our dating partners. We may think we know what deep love is, but our definitions may be strictly emotional and modern. Such definitions fall short in the crucible of marriage.

On the other hand, if both partners in a new marriage have

succeeded in this area, the opposite is true: They have no reason to think they will fail in marriage. In fact, they have strong assurance of ultimate success in marriage *as long as* they continue to practice self-sacrificing love at the deepest level.

It's exciting to know we can make progress whatever our present romantic involvement happens to be. Those who are already married can begin to apply Christian love skills in their marriage relationship and in other relationships as opportunities arise. Those who are seriously dating can begin to build intimate Christian relationships, not just with their dating partners, but especially with other people in non-romantic contexts. Those who are casually dating and those who are not dating at all can still build the skills for a successful marriage by simply learning the way of selfless love with their friends. Some of us will need to make new friends, which is no problem either. If these new friends include non-Christians, loving them will lead eventually to good opportunities for Christian witness.

When we stop focusing on *finding* the right person, and focus instead on *becoming* the right person, God begins to make profound changes in our relational lives!

Practical Steps Forward

Suppose your inventory reveals relatively little success so far in the area of mature relationships. Let's start with a worst-case scenario: You find that the people you know are more like acquaintances than friends. Even the casual definition is better than any non-dating relationships you can point to at the present time. What's your move?

Although this is not a book on forming friendships, the following schematic could provide some ideas on how to progress:

1. First, you will need to become convinced that deep personal relationships are necessary, good for you, enjoyable, good for others involved, and worth the effort. You should set out with genuine interest and desire, not as a forced exercise, duty, or requirement.

2. Once you have decided this, your next step is to learn to

establish rewarding casual friendships. Use the table in Chapter 3 as a road map to guide you into new friendships. Arrange to have *common experience* with other people who might become friends. For Christian relationships, a Bible study group or other Christian small group gathering would be a good place to begin. Don't expect to make friends if you are not willing to invest the time it takes to have regular social contact with other people who might become friends.

3. However, common experience is not enough. Next you should approach people and begin to explore their *personal inner working*. Ask appropriate questions to begin the sharing process and try to project positive feelings of interest, enthusiasm, and warmth as you do so. Avoid interrogation by sharing about your own inner working without focusing on yourself. Ask questions that are open rather than closed: "How do you feel about the victim's rights movement?" rather than "Have you heard of the victim's rights movement?" If you are able to take a genuine interest in others, relationships are almost sure to follow. Pray for the people you meet and talk to. What did you learn about their personal inner working? What questions occur to you based on that knowledge? Usually, subsequent conversations should build on what you have already learned. Before long, you will find new open doors for relationship, including casual friends. If, however, you are unable to make this work even after repeated attempts, there may be one or more barriers preventing further progress. Check the following chapters of this book, and if you need more help, don't hesitate to enlist the help of a Christian counselor or pastor.

4. Once you have casual friends, the next step is to seek to deepen one or two key friendships. Read again the description of *casual friendship* as described in Chapter 3. What is lacking in your casual friendships that could be added to enhance the relationship? You may need to schedule more common experience. Ask if you can join them in their favorite activities and learn to enjoy those activities yourself. While doing so, when appropriate, seek greater understanding of their personal inner working. Remember to be sensitive to the feedback you receive

from them. Don't push, but gradually and patiently gather understanding as they become willing to open up. Continue to pray for them, asking God to show you how you can bless them. Pray for ideas on how to affirm and show appreciation for them without becoming inappropriate, mushy, or "weird." Learn to enjoy the process of sensitively feeling your way into others' lives. What good can you do for them?

Sometimes simple, practical acts of service can thaw the ice in a relationship and open the way for more intimacy. My men's group had watched the pile of logs in my backyard sit for months unsplit. They heard me say casually that I didn't have time to get to it. One day, I came home from work and saw the whole pile split and neatly stacked. When I later found out it was two guys from my group, I was incredulous. "We had some time one afternoon and decided to take care of it," they explained. What a blessing! You can believe I looked at those guys with different eyes knowing their servant hearts. If we really want to love others, God will give us creative ways to serve them, like Christ washing the disciples' feet. That same servant attitude will go a long way toward success in our marriage.

5. After months or even years of investment with certain friends, you may find yourself entering into friendships that are relatively intimate. Such relationships usually have their own rewards, but there will also be times of intense irritation and even hurt. These times of testing are opportunities to learn the more advanced relational skills God will use in your marriage. You *will* be hurt by intimate friends. But are you willing, like Christ, to give yourself over to hurt for the sake of doing God's will? If not, you will have serious difficulties in your marriage. None of us should assume that our spouse won't hurt us! Or do we tell ourselves that we will forbear and work with the situation when it occurs in marriage but not when it occurs in friendships? Experience shows the opposite. On the other hand, if you are willing to be hurt for the sake of Christ, you can learn what it means to love others at the most intimate level, and you will become a person well suited to the challenges of a marriage relationship! There are, of course, times when the sacrificial

thing to do is to lay ourselves on the line to powerfully confront evil in our loved ones' lives. Whether God wants you to forbear or confront, you will learn more about how to keep and build successful relationships as long as you act for others' good in his name.

Examine your pattern for managing conflict in past and present friendships. Are you an appeaser? A compromiser? A competitor? An avoider? Any one of these might be appropriate in certain situations, but none of them can be appropriate in every situation. Conflict is a normal and even necessary part of any healthy relationship. The key is not to avoid conflict, but to conduct ourselves maturely during conflict. Read a book or two on conflict management from the Christian perspective, such as *The Peacemaker* by Ken Sande (Grand Rapids: Baker Book House), 1990; *Fight to the Better End* by Brian and Linda Jones (Wheaton, Ill.: SP Publications, Inc., 1989), or *Make Anger Your Ally* by Neil Clark Warren (Colorado Springs: Focus on the Family, 1993). Jones and Jones report that few spouses or even leaders of organizations have ever read even one book on conflict management—a definite oversight! For marital preparedness, every new bride or groom should carefully read at least two such books before taking their wedding vows.

FIVE

GROWING TOGETHER: MARRIAGE AND COMMUNITY

Love is the hardest lesson to learn in Christianity; but, for that reason, it should be most our care to learn it.

—WILLIAM PENN

In the triangle of love between ourselves, God, and other people is found the secret of existence, and the best foretaste, I suspect, that we can have on earth of what heaven will probably be like.

—SAMUEL M. SHOEMAKER

Brian and Cindy had been close friends with a number of people in their church, often enjoying personal fellowship in weekly home group meetings as well. When they started to date, things got hot and heavy fast. They were rarely seen apart from each other, and people generally felt awkward trying to talk to either one of them with the other always listening in. They were so "cemented together" people tended to feel they were intruding if they approached them.

Roommates who saw them coming into their respective apartments at all hours wondered whether the two were getting carried away, and Brian and Cindy were offended at the raised eyebrows they thought they saw. As a result, they gradually withdrew from the company of other Christian friends to be

67

with each other. Before long, their friends complained that they felt distant and uninvolved in Brian's and Cindy's lives.

They eventually got married and drifted even further from their former friends. For all practical purposes, they were completely out of Christian fellowship, except for cameo appearances from time to time.

Things didn't go well in their marriage. Nearly a year into it, Cindy was seen in tears at a Bible study, and she revealed that she and Brian were having trouble adjusting to married life. Brian also called unexpectedly, asking us for help. As it turned out, they had established some devastating patterns of failure in their relationship with each other. They had not managed their conflicts well, and an unexpected sexual problem had festered and become a huge wall between them. Communication had broken down after several awkward and embarrassing efforts at resolving the problem.

As responsible Christians, their former friends tried to help with counsel and support. But the same thought was on the minds of everyone involved: "Why did you wait until your problems grew to become monumental walls before seeking help?" In the discussions that followed, it became clear that both Brian and Cindy entertained some extremely immature and idealized expectations of what a marriage relationship should be. They had not drawn on the wisdom of longtime married Christians who could have spared them much pain. Their marriage eventually took years of gradual growth to recover. Now Brian and Cindy are vigorous advocates for couples staying involved in the body of Christ during engagement and marriage.

Unfortunately, this story is not unusual. Far too many newly married couples struggle in isolation and confusion during the early phase of marriage because they discount the importance of Christian community in building a Christian family. Our study of distressed marriages in our own church revealed that rocky and failed marriages usually occur among those who are on the fringes of Christian community. A vital, deep bond with other Christians is one of the keys to successful marriage.

Family and Community

In Romans 12:1 Paul urges us to ". . . make a decisive dedication of your bodies—presenting all your members and faculties—as a living sacrifice . . . to God, which is your reasonable service . . ." (The Amplified Bible). If we believe God exists, nothing less than complete commitment to him is reasonable. Our Creator should be our source, our ultimate destiny, and our present integration point. Although reason tells us this, Paul is emphasizing something else. He bases his call for commitment on "the mercies of God," which he has expounded in chapters 1–11. Since God has demonstrated through Christ that he is a loving God, his will for our lives must also be "good and acceptable and perfect" (v. 2). Why, then, wouldn't we want to make him and his will the top priority in our lives?

But there's more. Immediately following this statement in Romans 12:1, Paul declares in verse 5 that "we who are many are one Body in Christ, and individually members of one another." The body of Christ refers to the Church. Since we are "in Christ," and therefore members of the body of Christ, a commitment to Christ is also a commitment to his body. If we claim we are fully committed to Christ, but remain uncommitted to the body of Christ, we are fundamentally confused. We have failed to take into account that our position in him includes a position in his body.

Appropriate involvement in the local expression of Christ's body should be a major priority in our lives.

The Local Church

In the New Testament, commitment to the body of Christ is pictured not as a general commitment to the universal Church, but rather as a vital functional and relational link to Christian brothers and sisters in a local community. Both in Romans 12 and in the parallel passages in 1 Corinthians 12 and 14, the local, not the universal, body of Christ is in view. This is clear since both passages focus on the effect of each member's spiritual gifts on the life of the group.

Paul also says, ". . . the eye cannot say to the hand, 'I have no need of you'" (1 Corinthians 12:21). In other words, we cannot ignore our need for the other members of a local church. We may survive as Christians without the help of others, but our Christian walk will be needlessly impoverished. Some Christians today fail to deeply understand the role the body of Christ should play in their lives. Modern individualism and the drift of many traditional churches away from being a committed community, like that in the New Testament, have combined to produce confusion. Yet this passage and others teach that in-depth involvement in Christian fellowship is *indispensable* for Christian growth.

The input that God intends to supply to us through other Christians is so vital that it would be pointless to expect spiritual growth beyond the most rudimentary levels without it. Few would be foolish enough to think they could grow without regular prayer or Bible study. But the Bible speaks of body-life in similar terms. Like prayer, body-life is a means of growth. If we know we can't grow without prayer, we should also know we can't grow without consistent, in-depth Christian fellowship.

> *Koinonia* is more than attending one or two meetings a week. It is authentically sharing the life of Christ with one another.

Attendance Versus *Koinonia*

What is Christian fellowship? The New Testament often uses the word *koinonia*, which is usually translated "fellowship" or "sharing." The word means "to have in common" or "to share." In the New Testament God repeatedly exhorts us to share the life of Christ with one another in the body of Christ. This is not possible in any other context. We share the life of Christ when we share his love with other Christians through

70

relationships and our spiritual gifts. (Some passages that merit study in this are Acts 2:42; Romans 12:4–16; 1 Corinthians 12 and 14; Galatians 6:2; Ephesians 4:11–16; 5:18–21; Philippians 2:1–5; Colossians 2:19; 3:12–17; 1 Thessalonians 5:14; Hebrews 3:13; 10:24–25; James 5:16; and 1 John 1:3.)[1] The act of exchanging, or sharing (*koinonia*), God's love is called "ministry." Ministry simply means "service."

The biblical terms ministry, *koinonia*, fellowship, gifts, and sharing all describe the active practice of serving love in a committed Christian community. Such sharing, along with the other means of growth such as prayer, Bible study, and the discipline of the Holy Spirit, is the lifeblood of growing Christians.

Koinonia is much more than attending one or two meetings a week. Teachers today often stress the importance of attending church by quoting Hebrews 10:25: ". . . not forsaking our own assembling together . . ." Many take the verse to mean that only our presence at church meetings is necessary. But the important point is not just that we attend meetings (although this is a necessary part), but that we authentically share the life of Christ with one another.

According to 1 Corinthians 12:21, ". . . the eye cannot say to the hand, 'I have no need of you.'" In other words, we need not just the *presence* of the other members but also their *function*. The reason our eyes cannot say they don't need our hands is that eyes cannot feel or work—only hands can do that. The biblical picture of the body of Christ teaches us that the local church should be much more than a few Christian meetings. It should be an organic union based on genuine personal relationships and mutual interdependence. As Paul puts it, ". . . speaking the truth in love, we are to grow up in all aspects into Him, who is the Head, even Christ . . ." (Ephesians 4:15).

No part of our physical body exists merely to be nourished and sustained by the rest of the body. Rather, each part has a distinct function that it alone can provide. Imagine your hand refusing to do anything! This would be like a Christian who looks for a church for the sole purpose of "meeting my needs." *Koinonia* means that we also participate in a way that meets oth-

71

ers' needs. God has arranged the body of Christ so that we must depend on others' gifts while they depend on ours in true interdependence. (See 1 Corinthians 12:17–18.)

Imperatives for Today

If *koinonia* is to be more than a slogan, we will need to be close enough to other Christians to know each other's needs. Most spiritual gifts described in the Bible, whether they involve counseling, encouragement, service, or teaching, require personal knowledge of those we serve, at least to the extent that we understand their needs. We also need a level of relationship that promotes trust and open sharing. No wonder the early church commonly practiced more or less daily involvement in some sort of Christian fellowship. (See Acts 2:42–47.) This is what Paul calls ". . . being fitted and held together by that which every joint supplies, according to the proper working of each individual part . . ." (Ephesians 4:16).

Unfortunately, such personal interdependence is often lacking in Christian churches. "Fellowship" is the name of the hall across from the sanctuary rather than a lifestyle of sharing Christ's life with one another. In this environment, church members learn to relate to each other superficially, and are therefore unequipped to help each other with the very painful problems we all have.

A few years ago, George got involved in our church seeking help for serious sexual problems that threatened his marriage. Since he had been serving as a deacon of his former evangelical church, we asked him why he didn't seek help from his pastor and fellow deacons. He replied that when he disclosed these sin problems to his pastor, he advised George to come to our church because we were "used to helping people with your kind of problem." We were glad to try to help him, but we lamented the fact that this kind of involvement was regarded as unusual in the Christian community.

Marriage and family relationships belong in the context of the Christian community. In Ephesians 5, marital roles are defined in the context of relations with the community, and even depend on those relationships. (Chapter 11 includes a more detailed discussion of this passage and its implications for marriage.) We should accept our need for counsel and support from our Christian community both before and during our married lives.

> The modern view is, "You respect me by not questioning any of my views or actions."

Sometimes couples, like Brian and Cindy, take an unbiblical, autonomous attitude toward marriage. "It's none of the church's business!" is the cry of the autonomous dating or married couple. Such a cry may be appropriate for some private areas in marriage, but as a whole, it misses the mark. By walling off such a central area of our lives, we have rendered the concept of *koinonia* a dead letter.

Modern Relational Theories

People in the modern world, in their interpersonal alienation, have made the notion of unqualified, radical privacy the central value in human relationships. But as thirst for privacy and autonomy increases, closeness with others decreases. In place of closeness, the modern world has accepted the hollow value of being "respected." And according to most modern people, you respect me by not questioning any of my views or actions. The result is the farthest thing possible from the biblical picture of interdependent love. We are reduced to people who circle each other warily, at a great distance, snarling and protecting ourselves from being offended.

Modern alienated theories about human relationships also carry over into marriage. No wonder marriage is failing in the modern world! Today's contempt for authority leads people to call for unqualified privacy. But we may miss key correctives based on the resident wisdom in the church. Any time we open up about our marriages to other trusted Christian friends, they may point out some aspect of our relationship that runs contrary to God's will. But this is exactly what God intends.

In the modern world, to "respect" each other, we must affirm that each person knows what is best and needs no advice from us. But God recognizes no internal guidance system that renders all of our individual or cultural views correct. Many of us have learned some terribly false views, and these views need to be exposed to the light of the Truth, not just respected. God knows our Christian friends can help us do this. He believes we need counsel and admonition from others because we may be deceived or blind. This is why Paul says, "I myself am convinced, my brothers, that you yourselves are full of goodness, complete in knowledge and competent to instruct one another" (Romans 15:14, NIV).

The desire to have everyone mind their own business is incompatible with the idea of relational closeness in the church as pictured in the New Testament. We need to realize that our urges toward autonomy and selfishness are not diseases we catch like swine flu; these are sins that should be confronted and changed.

> The desire to have everyone "mind their own business" is incompatible with the idea of relational closeness.

Achieving good relationships within the body of Christ takes work and time. Ideally, such relationships should be a prerequisite to Christian marriage. Even serious dating is less than it could be when Christian couples are not involved in authentic *koinonia*. If our local church is not interested in *koinonia*, we should find some like-minded Christians who will join us in forming a small fellowship group within the church. If this isn't possible, we should consider finding a church more interested in promoting deep fellowship.

Unfortunately, many couples lose their former depth of involvement in Christian community when they begin dating seriously. Like Brian and Cindy, they fail to see *koinonia* as an important component of a healthy romantic relationship. In immature romance relationships, couples can only focus on each other and consequently lose interest in other relationships. Sometimes couples conclude that "no one can understand what we are going through." Couples in love may feel their emotional needs are fully met and therefore they no longer need regular or deep *koinonia*. This type of withdrawal often signals a hyper-dependent relationship, which will be fragile in the future.

For whatever reason, withdrawal from fellowship is both wrong and dangerous because it deprives a couple of counsel and support from mature Christians at the very time they need it most. Later, when they return for help at a time of crisis, they have lost the relationships they need for in-depth sharing. To avoid this, dating couples should exert their energies to maintain their other relationships in fellowship before marriage, even if it means a little less time alone together.

Dating couples who withdraw from fellowship are also withdrawing their important contribution to others. Such couples should ask themselves, "Is it possible that we were involved with other Christians only for what we could receive until we found our 'true love'?" This attitude is selfish and is sure to cause problems in the dating relationship as well as any future marriage.

The Role of Counsel

Few decisions are as important as the decision to get married. As followers of Christ, we should want to know if our decision is in accordance with God's will for our lives. For this reason, we should pray and reflect before making marriage plans. The Bible declares that wise people also seek spiritual counsel when making important decisions. (See Proverbs 11:14; 12:15; 15:22; 19:20; 20:5, 18; and 24:6.) Here, too, we need to discover the importance of the body of Christ.

Today, many people have experienced living in a cult or an

authoritarian church. Such groups may have tried to minimize the significance of individual decision making by dominating every area of their members' lives. Authoritarian groups often abuse biblical concepts such as "shepherding" and "accountability" to justify intruding into people's private lives. Some groups have actually tried to tell their members whom they should marry. Christ, on the other hand, stresses the significance of the individual, including freedom of choice. In John 10:3 Jesus says the good shepherd "calls his own sheep by name." God deals with us as individuals as well as part of a group, and even with all his authority, God does not force us to comply with his wishes.

The worst reaction one can have to an experience with an authoritarian group is to deny the value of mature Christians' discernment and counsel in life-changing decisions. In the marriage ceremony, we ask the church to stand as witnesses and supporters of our commitment to each other. This request should also be coupled with the willingness to have members of the body of Christ counsel us about our marriage decisions. Remember, their counsel is just that—counsel. It is not a binding "word from the Lord" or a "chain of authority" that must be obeyed. Such binding authority should be reserved for the Word of God as revealed in Scripture.

Any time we don't care about the input of other mature Christians—any time we only want to "do our own thing"—we are in trouble spiritually. Such an attitude demonstrates a dangerous disregard for God's will. Often we are blind to the fruit we have borne since beginning a romantic relationship. We may need to hear some criticism about the way we have handled ourselves. Remember, the whole point of being deceived is that we don't realize we are deceived. If others are critical, we should try to understand their reasons, especially if the critics are mature Christians.

Family Life in the Community of God

In addition to the wisdom we gain from other Christians, our marriage itself will be stabilized and matured through vital involvement in the local church. God does not intend families to live on their own without outside support. Although it comes as a surprise to modern secular culture, the nuclear family is not an island fortress able to meet all its own needs.

Frank and Nancy discovered this fact in the nick of time. When their three-year-old son died suddenly and inexplicably, their lives were shattered. Since Nancy was not a Christian and Frank did not know how to walk with Christ, they simply did not have the spiritual resources to help each other through this agonizing experience. Their non-Christian friends and family members shared their grief but could not provide them with the spiritual support and insight they so desperately needed. As their marriage began to buckle under the strain, they feared they were on their way to joining the huge proportion of couples who divorce following the death of their young children.

But by God's grace, Nancy came to Christ, and Frank recommitted his life to Christ. They also became deeply involved in Christian fellowship by joining a home fellowship group operated by our church. Through this group, they received Christ's love and support as they grieved over the loss of their son. To make matters worse, Nancy suffered through three miscarriages. Their Christian friends provided meals, house-cleaning, and baby-sitting. They also prayed for them, taught them the biblical view of suffering, and offered them counsel. In spite of their grief, Frank and Nancy began to serve others in Christian love.

In this context, they gradually began to experience the fulfillment of God's promise that he is able to work for good in all things to those who love him (Romans 8:28). Today their marriage is stronger than ever, and two relatives cited the support they saw from Frank and Nancy's Christian friends as a major factor in their own conversions to Christ. Their story is one of many that underscores the importance of Christian fellowship in marriage.

Many Christian couples have discovered the stabilizing effect that consistent *koinonia* has on a marriage. Such support is available to those who have sufficient closeness with others to allow mutual sharing and counseling within marriage. Only when we have built close relationships with Christian friends will we feel comfortable discussing marriage issues. Struggling with problems in a new marriage can be scary, especially when we are unable to share our problems with any wise and trustworthy fellow-believers. But the time to begin laying the foundation for this sort of trust is before marriage.

Learning and practicing *koinonia* before marriage also usually enables us to establish a personal ministry. This advantage is so significant that we devote the following chapter to it.

Notes

1. For an in-depth and practical analysis of the passages, see Gary De-Lashmutt, *Loving God's Way: A Fresh Look at the "One Another" Passages* (Grand Rapids: Kregel Publications, 1996).

SIX

COMPETENT TO GIVE: MARRIAGE AND MINISTRY

Instead of allowing yourself to be so unhappy, just let your love grow as God wants it to grow; love more persons more; love them more unselfishly, without thought of return. The return, never fear, will take care of itself.

—HENRY DRUMMOND

There is more pleasure in loving than in being beloved.

—THOMAS FULLER

Few things promote successful marriages more than involvement in Christian ministry. But in spite of its importance, the concept of ministry remains nebulous for many Christians.

Our Marriage Study

In 1981, we were pastoring a young church that was emerging from college into adulthood. Scores of couples were getting married every year, and before long marriage problems began to surface. Our board of elders was alarmed to discover that many marriages were in serious trouble. We felt we had to do something to stem the tide of apparent failure in marriage.

We launched a study of marriage success in the church. We listed couples we knew, and then filled in descriptive fields for

79

things such as age at time of marriage, age in the Lord, previous marriages, cohabitation, and many others. We also rated the marriages ranging from those separated or divorced, to those who were seriously distressed, to those who were adjusting well.

We were surprised when we analyzed the correlations. One thing stood out as correlating with good adjustment in marriage more than anything else. We would have guessed age in the Lord or family background would be the clearest factors in success. Instead, the clearest factor, by a significant margin, was involvement in defined Christian ministry before marriage!

The more we thought about these results, the more sense they made. Christian counselors find that the same factors that prevent Christians from developing an effective ministry also interfere with their ability to succeed in marriage. Success in ministry requires the ability to work with others, consistency, self-discipline, commitment, concern for others, and self-sacrifice. These are the same elements we need to succeed in marriage. We have no reason to believe we will suddenly do within marriage what we have not already learned to do before marriage. Only a proven ability to victoriously serve and build up others will assure that we have the skills needed when serving our spouses.

What Is Ministry?

Ministry means serving others for the sake of Christ, either to help them begin a saving relationship with Christ or to help them grow in that relationship. Christians practice ministry because we believe our Christianity is not just for our own benefit, but also for the benefit of others. Those who practice transcendental meditation do so for their own benefit. Christianity is completely different in this respect. We receive blessing from God, but immediately, the next goal is to turn around and give away what we have received. Paul says,

Do nothing from selfishness or empty conceit, but with

humility of mind let each of you regard one another as more important than himself (Philippians 2:3).

Let each of you please his neighbor for his good, to his edification (Romans 15:2).

The New Testament unambiguously teaches that ministry is the birthright of every Christian. The passages mentioned in the previous chapter regarding the body of Christ affirm that every Christian has a distinct role in the body. In 1 Corinthians 12:4–6, Paul teaches that the Spirit gives Christians *gifts, ministries,* and *effects.* God gives spiritual gifts to "each one individually just as He wills" (v. 11). This use of the word "each" implies "each and every," meaning that all Christians have at least one spiritual gift. A ministry, in this context, is the sphere in which we use our gifts. Therefore, if all Christians have gifts, God must intend that they all have ministries as well. This point is clear from the highlighted words in the following verse:

But speaking the truth in love, we are to grow up in all aspects into Him, who is the head, even Christ, from whom the whole body, being fitted and held together by *that which every joint supplies,* according to the proper *working of each individual part,* causes the growth of the body for the building up of itself in love (Ephesians 4:15–16, emphasis added).

Here the metaphor of the body of Christ teaches that every one of us has a contribution, which constitutes our ministry.

Why Ministry Prepares for Marriage

Ministry is a word that originally meant "service." Therefore, in the New Testament, the issue of ministry is very close to the key concept of Christian love or "serving love." Both involve serving others for their good. This is why Paul stresses Christian love in the middle of his discussion of gifts and ministries in 1 Corinthians 13. Both ministry and serving love, to be effective, must be practiced with consistency, competence, and self-sacrifice. Therefore we should not be surprised to learn that our involvement in Christian ministry has a bearing on the ease with which we succeed in marriage. Since marriage is a type of ministry, the more experience we have had in authentic Christian ministry, the more likely we will be to succeed in marriage.

Assessing Our Ministries

When assessing whether we have developed adequate ministry skills, the following checklist should help.

Ministry Should Be Concrete

Many Christians will drop a word of encouragement here or there, or help set up chairs for a meeting. But these acts of "ministry on the fly," while real and good, are not the types that prepare us to succeed in marriage. Marriage is much more a matter of daily, consistent, and committed servitude. Therefore, only concrete, or well-defined, ministry will give us the preparation we need.

What is concrete, or well-defined, ministry? Our ministry is concrete when we are involved with, and responsible for, specific people and tasks. We need not be able to identify all our spiritual gifts, but we should know what our areas of responsibility are. Knowing all our spiritual gifts could take years, but establishing a concrete ministry is possible much sooner.

If we have been unable to establish a defined ministry in this sense even though we are years old in the Lord, our inability may contain a warning. Failure to establish concrete ministry may betray a lack of initiative in seeking out needs. If so, such passivity will usually translate into passivity in marriage. Couples are often aware of one another's needs, but lack the initiative to do anything about it. Both partners sit like two frogs on a log, waiting for the other to take initiative, often despairing at the same time. What's wrong with this picture?

Often, unless we have had practice in the area of taking initiative to meet needs, we simply don't know how to get outside ourselves to serve others. Ministry experience could help correct such a tendency.

Sometimes we have not been able to establish concrete ministry because, though we perceive needs in others and want to help, we simply don't know how to meet those needs. Again, such a lack of knowledge will probably be a problem within marriage. Only an inquiring and learning mind in the area of meeting needs is ready for the challenge of marriage. Regular experience in Christian ministry is one of the best ways to develop knowledge about meeting others' needs.

Some of us have failed to establish concrete ministry because we lack the humility necessary to meet what seem to be "routine" needs in people. If we are only willing to practice Christian service when it is glorified or noticed by others, it suggests we have an ego problem. For some,

> **Ministry passivity will usually translate into marriage passivity.**

ministry is not a way to serve others, but a path to self-aggrandizement. Any such ego problem will present a serious peril in marriage, where so many needs are "routine."

Ministry Should Include the Personal

While the church often needs impersonal or practical service like fixing cars, house-cleaning, and so on, Christians should also seek involvement in personal ministry relationships. This is particularly true for those considering marriage. Those who consistently avoid personal ministry may lack the ability to relate intimately with people. We discussed this problem in Chapters 2 and 3.

We Should Be Able to Minister Separately

Dating couples should raise additional questions if they want to be sure they have maximized their ministry experience. First, are they able to minister separately? Or is one of them strong in ministry, while the other only attempts ministry when

83

together with the stronger partner? Such an arrangement could mean that the weaker partner is overly dependent, reflecting insufficient confidence in his or her own spiritual maturity, or even something worse. Perhaps the one who never ministers apart from the other is not really as interested in serving God as in being together with a loved one.

Inequality based on lack of confidence can create problems in marriage because one spouse may not have the courage to address problems in the other's life. At the same time, the more dominant partner may develop disrespect, leading to friction.

When one partner secretly lacks genuine interest in ministry, a more serious problem is predictable. Those who are interested in ministry only because it allows them to be near their loved ones will lose this interest after marriage. They no longer lack for time together with their

> We should not lose our life priorities the moment our loved one enters the room.

spouse, as they did when dating, so ministry loses whatever value it once had. These couples may end up "unequally yoked" in the area of ministry, which leads to friction and heartache for both. (In the next chapter we will discuss the ultimate form of unequal yoking: marriage between a Christian and a non-Christian.)

We Should Be Able to Minister When Together

Other couples are able to minister when apart, but not when they are together. Some couples instantly focus only on one another whenever they enter each other's presence. While this kind of relationship may be cute in high school, it looks different with adults. Exclusive or obsessive love often indicates the couple needs to grow and mature for a while until they gain more balance in their relationship. Sometimes the hyper-dependent fervor for one another signals a codependent or idealized type of love that may crash down with terrible disappointment. We should not lose our life priorities the moment our loved one enters the room.

Some couples have problems communicating, cooperating, or submitting to each other in ministry situations; therefore, they only engage in Christian service when their partners are absent. This may not seem serious while dating, but it signals the presence of problems that could be catastrophic in marriage.

Building Our Ministries

No activity will bear more positive fruit in our lives while we are waiting to be married than developing a defined personal ministry. Even if we have no prospect in sight for marriage in the near future, ministry will help prepare us for marriage. We may safely suppose that no path leads to marriage more surely than becoming the type of person who is ready for marriage. Even if God elects to take us another direction as lifelong singles, none of our effort will be wasted.

How can you develop a personal ministry? Most Christians can accomplish important spiritual work for God through sharing Christ and discipling young Christians. Ministries of mercy, where we take care of the weak or disabled, and counsel or encourage those in need, are also common areas to check. Hopefully, your church offers training that will help members develop ministry. If not, you have to decide whether to attempt establishing a ministry through personal initiative, or finding a church or organization that will help. Assuming the church is a suitable environment for ministry, and will either help, or at least not oppose the efforts of its members to build ministry relationships, the following ideas should help.

First, beginning to minister in areas that fit your spiritual gifts will significantly strengthen your experience with ministry. You can get help identifying your areas of potential gifting from several existing sources.[1]

Next, knowledge about ministry comes from three primary sources: the Word of God (including books written about the Word), more mature Christians, and the direct teaching of the

Holy Spirit as we practice. As you make attempts to serve others, you may need to seek guidance when you encounter needs you don't know how to meet. You should identify people with proven knowledge in your area of ministry and either obtain their advice or, better still, observe them at work. Meeting typical needs in others can become a powerful learning experience. Only in the laboratory of life can we directly apply the truths of God's Word to life experience.

As our ability to help others increases, we will develop a taste and an appetite for giving our lives away to others. This often results in a revolution of priorities and profound spiritual growth. At the same time, we are learning how to recognize and help others with their problems and needs—invaluable skills in marriage.

The Non-Ministering Couple

Immature couples often completely fail to establish a ministry ethic before or during their marriages. Such couples form a cozy "love nest" and ignore the needs of those around them. Their nest may look loving, but such "love" is really a form of corporate selfishness, quite alien from the dynamic self-giving love taught by Christ. Jesus said, "If you love those who love you, what reward will you get? Are not even the tax collectors doing that?" (Matthew 5:46, NIV). Any family that only loves itself is falling woefully short of the biblical picture of healthy Christian living. Instead, marriage should *improve* our ability to give to others. Paul says, ". . . God was reconciling the world to himself in Christ, not counting men's sins against them. And he has committed to us the message of reconciliation" (2 Corinthians 5:19, NIV). This is exciting news. We are not here merely to be reconciled to God, but also to be the agents of reconciliation for lost millions around us. Plan on making this purpose a central feature in your marriage. You won't regret it.

Ministry Within Marriage

Involvement in ministry, when properly balanced with other areas of life, nearly always strengthens a Christian marriage. This is true for several reasons. First, a commitment to self-giving ministry will help to combat selfishness in our marriage relationship. It does this by providing regular practice in giving, while regularly confronting Christian workers with their areas of selfishness that interfere with ministry. Second, if both partners are involved in ministry, it becomes an important area of common ground in the marriage. The couple can work together toward common ministry goals. Finally, this commitment to ministry provides an outward purpose for marriage beyond self-satisfaction.

Some Christian thinkers have even suggested that the best time to get married is when two people feel that both will be more effective for Christ married than single. Such an outward purpose and shared goal should have a noticeable cementing effect on the marriage. These benefits should not surprise us, since the Bible indicates that ministry is a means of growth, just like prayer, Bible study, and fellowship.[2]

Notes

1. See Kenneth C. Kinghorn, *Discovering Your Spiritual Gifts* (Grand Rapids: Francis Asbury Press, 1981); Bruce L. Bugbee, *Networking* (Pasadena: Charles E. Fuller Institute, 1991); Robert E. Logan and Janet Logan, *Spiritual Gifts Implementation: Moving From Gifts Discovery to Ministry Placement* (Pasadena: Fuller Evangelistic Association, 1986).
2. Although the need for the Bible, prayer, and fellowship are well taught in the modern church, the role of ministry is often overlooked. The following passages either teach or imply that ministry is a means of growth. Note that the blessing is not just for those receiving service, but also (and especially) for those giving it. Colossians 2:19; John 4:34; 13:12–17, 34–35; Philippians 2:1–4; Acts 20:35; Romans 12:10–13; Hebrews 10:24–25; 1 Corinthians 12–13; 1 John 3:16-18.

SEVEN

BUILDING ON A SOLID FOUNDATION

A good marriage is not a contract between two persons but a sacred covenant between three.

—DONALD T. KAUFMAN

Love does not consist in gazing at each other but in looking together in the same direction.

—ANTOINE DE SAINT-EXUPÉRY

In a successful Christian marriage, both spouses have vital personal relationships with God and the ability to share this relationship with each other. As we discussed in Chapter 2, the scriptural basis for this comes, in part, from the fact that a marriage is a community of believers. Therefore, the biblical patterns for *koinonia* apply to marriage just as they would to any Christian group. Since our spouses are our brothers or sisters in Christ, all of the principles dealing with edification within the body of Christ also should be a part of our relationship at home. It may seem unnecessary to say that dating couples should get started in developing this aspect of their relationship through sharing prayer, Bible study, and fellowship with each other. Unfortunately, experience shows that otherwise strong Christian couples often neglect this area while dating.

Reasons for Neglect

Sometimes their lack of spiritual maturity explains why couples neglect this area of the relationship. The two people may not have learned yet how to nourish and sustain their own individual walks with Christ, let alone how to integrate their dating relationship around their relationship with Christ.

With other couples, worldly attitudes dominate the relationship and adversely affect its spiritual vitality. Some Christians are actually embarrassed by their commitment to Christ and actively seek to hide it from their partners. Others secretly want to share spiritually but are unwilling to jeopardize the relationship by making it an issue. Guilt feelings stemming from inappropriate sexual conduct may also stifle interest in spiritual sharing. Still other couples are just too lazy to put forth the effort to build common spiritual ground.

Many dating couples erroneously believe that positive spiritual habits will be easier to develop after they are married. In fact, the opposite is often true. Married couples commonly report that prayer and spiritual fellowship *decrease* in marriage. This may be because, as the novelty wears off, couples feel less need to cultivate their relationship, including its spiritual dimension.

Building Shared Spirituality

For all of these reasons, Christian couples should take decisive steps to build habits in the area of spiritual sharing early. The easiest time to introduce this kind of sharing is at the beginning of a romantic relationship. Otherwise, we tend to establish the relationship on a non-spiritual foundation, and this can be very difficult to change later. Of course, even though it may be difficult, we can develop spiritual sharing in the relationship at any time, before or after marriage. If both people are sincere in their commitment to Christ, and if they are willing to take practical steps like those explained below, they can reorient their relationship so that it centers around the Lord. But the easiest and most natural time to lay this foundation is at the beginning of the relationship.

What are some practical steps that will help put Christ in the center where he belongs? The following checklist should help.

Encourage Independent Growth

First, both partners should actively encourage each other in their personal spiritual growth, even when this means sacrificing time with each other. Nothing is more spiritually deadening than hyper-dependent relationships where those involved aren't allowed to spend time with peers developing relationships and participating in Bible study, prayer, and ministry. Possessive and controlling love is selfish love, and it will quickly short-circuit spiritual growth for both partners in the relationship. Those who control their loved ones are betraying a form of idolatry where they look to another human being to supply what only Christ can deliver. The ones who submit to this control also suffer spiritually as their support systems and friendships wither from neglect.

Spiritual sharing only with one another is insufficient, as we discussed earlier, and will result in a relationship that eventually implodes into selfishness. Although counselors worry about some married couples who use fellowship or ministry as an excuse to avoid intimacy, this is rarely seen among dating couples.

> Possessive and controlling love is selfish love, and it will quickly short-circuit spiritual growth for both partners in the relationship.

When our loved ones actively pursue spiritual growth independently, we should see their pursuit as a blessing and encourage it. We should view any resulting sacrifice as an important investment in the health of our relationship rather than as a threat to it.

Regular Scheduled Time

Most couples need to set aside at least weekly time to share, study, or pray together. Positive habits are rarely built without a commitment to incorporate them into our weekly schedule. When we try to catch some time for spiritual sharing "on the fly," we usually wind up with little time spent. Instead, we should establish a consistent habit of spending even a few minutes in regular spiritual sharing. Then if we want to, we can gradually lengthen the time we spend. This is better than setting an unrealistic goal and then quitting because we get frustrated or bored.

We should not be surprised or discouraged if this kind of sharing is awkward at first. Some awkwardness is normal, especially at first. The notion that "we should wait until it comes naturally" is mistaken. Unfortunately, that day will probably never come. Rather, as we continue to pray and study and share together, it will gradually become more natural and fulfilling. Try reading New Testament books together, or good books on Christian living. Some devotional books or even books like this one can become richer when shared together with one you love.

Seek to Balance Each Other

Couples should use their spiritual strengths to help each other. Usually, vital Christians find that they have an affinity for certain areas of spiritual living and an aversion for others. For example, one person may enjoy Bible study but have trouble with prayer, while the other person may be just the opposite. This should be a source of help, not friction. We need to agree to learn from each other how to improve in our weak areas. Such cooperation builds both partners' individual walks with Christ while strengthening the very important spiritual "partnership" aspect of the relationship.

Mutual Respect and Patience

We should be gracious and avoid patronizing or intimidating our loved one when sharing. We will often need to use basic ministry skills to engender interest and motivation in our partner. Clearly, the ability to work with people in ministry would be very helpful here, as we discussed in Chapter 6.

Include Spontaneous Sharing

Spontaneous opportunities for spiritual sharing, such as long drives, or when crisis strikes, can be turned into times of fellowship, prayer, or listening to and discussing a teaching tape. When married, these spontaneous times of spiritual sharing are important for our children to observe because they see that our Christian walk permeates our lives rather than being reserved only for meetings.

Build Common Ministry

Building common areas of ministry should make it easier and more natural to engage in spiritual sharing, as suggested in Chapter 6. For married couples with children, this should definitely include sharing the privilege and responsibility of nurturing and instructing our children in the Lord. Shared spiritual goals lead to healthy sharing and support.

What About Resistance?

We all have certain times when we don't feel like praying or sharing. But when one partner is consistently reluctant to share spiritually, we are confronted with a warning. First, ask this question: Is the reluctance only there with me, or also with other people? If the reluctant partner is able to share spiritual things with other Christians but not with his or her spouse, the problem may be *how* the couple relates to each other in this area. Lack of grace or undue pressure can cast a chill on our spiritual relationships. So too can unresolved conflicts. Tensions in our relationships, including sexual problems, may result in alienation and decreased communication.

However, when one partner is consistently reluctant to

share spiritually, not only with the other partner, but with anyone, the person almost certainly has a values or attitude problem in his or her spiritual life. Whatever the cause, such reluctance signals a very serious problem. For a dating couple to proceed into marriage without first resolving such a problem would be a grave and unwise risk. Why assume that a person you plan to marry will ever change in this area if he or she hasn't done so already? If we are thinking of marrying someone based on future spiritual potential, we should ask ourselves, "Why has

> Why assume that a person you plan to marry will ever change in the spiritual area if he or she hasn't done so already?

the potential not yet been realized?" We should be willing to go as far as losing marriage opportunities because we insist on a spiritual basis for that relationship.

The Ox and Mule Syndrome

To seriously date or to consider marrying a non-Christian is outside the will of God. In 2 Corinthians 6:14–15, Paul says, "Do not be bound together with unbelievers, for . . . what has a believer in common with an unbeliever?"

The verb "bound together" literally means "unequally yoked." Paul is recalling the Old Testament command in Deuteronomy 22:10, "You shall not plow with an ox and a donkey together." God forbade yoking together beasts of such diverse sizes and strengths because the excessive chafing of the yoke would injure both animals. In the same way, Paul says that a binding relationship between a Christian and a non-Christian will be mutually injurious because they are so essentially different.

Of course, some marriages eventually become centered around God when the non-believing spouse later comes to

94

Christ. However, for every instance where an unequally yoked marriage recovers in this way, there are a dozen tragedies. When a true Christian marries a non-Christian, there is almost certainly great suffering ahead. Christians who violate God's will in this way have based their marriage relationships around something or someone other than Christ. They have compromised their relationship with God.

We can be thankful that God will not reject us for such lapses in judgment. But, as we discussed before, he has never promised to preserve us from pain when we defy his will. Besides the pain we will likely bear from such a decision, compromising our faith suggests that Jesus Christ is not the most important Person in our life. This will hardly increase our non-Christian spouse's respect for our faith.

> **No matter how "right" a relationship feels, God's will concerning seriously dating or marrying a non-Christian will not change.**

More importantly, there is no reason to believe that a non-Christian (or a "Christian" who is uninterested in the things of God) will change after marriage. The record shows that this rarely happens, and the Bible pointedly reminds us that God gives us no such assurance. Paul asks of mixed partners in 1 Corinthians 7:16, ". . . how do you know, O wife, whether you will save your husband? Or how do you know, O husband, whether you will save your wife?"

Remember, we are free to choose whom we marry, but we are also responsible for the possible lifelong consequences. How easily we can say, "I'm ready to accept that responsibility," until we experience the painful results of ignoring God's will! Often an unequally yoked person returns to follow God closely years later and faces stiff opposition from a non-Christian spouse. Even worse, unequally yoked believers may permanently compromise their commitment to Christ in order to keep peace in the home. Children also invariably suffer in such marriages.

Considering the clear biblical teaching against marrying non-Christians, Christians need to be honest with themselves when they consider entering, or continuing, a romantic relationship of this sort. Embarking on such a relationship, they are really denying that God knows best how to bring fulfillment into their lives, and that he is committed to their good. (See Matthew 7:11 and Deuteronomy 10:13.) Such a denial constitutes a betrayal of what we say we believe about God: that he is our wise and loving heavenly Father who always seeks our good.

Before going ahead, ask yourself: What evidence can you find that God has ever been wrong or unloving in his dealings with you? When have you ever regretted, in any lasting way, following God's will? Why would this issue be any different?

No matter how "right" a relationship feels, God's will concerning seriously dating or marrying a non-Christian will not change. If you find yourself drawn toward such a situation, resolve now to obey God despite the cost. Any delay only makes the decision harder. Even though you may feel terrible pain for a while, you will look back later and realize this decision was one of the best you ever made. We have never met a Christian who wishes he or she had gone ahead into marriage with their non-Christian dating partner. But we have met scores of miserable Christians who would do anything if they could go back and change their decision to marry a non-Christian or a disinterested Christian. Seek out an older Christian for advice and support as you trust God. You'll be thankful sooner than you think!

For a variety of reasons, many Christians find themselves married to a non-Christian, or a so-called Christian, who demonstrates no desire to grow in Christ. Although God does not promise that such a spouse will change, he *does* promise he will be at work in all things for good for those who love him (Romans 8:28). God is able to work through these situations to cause growth and bring glory to himself *if we respond properly*. If you are in this situation, consider the following suggestions.

Admit Fault

You should acknowledge before God your own responsibility for your current problems. When you do this, you are reassuming a position of honesty and humility in your relationship with God, which must be your foundation. Remember that God "is opposed to the proud, but gives grace to the humble. Submit therefore to God. . . . Draw near to God and he will draw near to you" (James 4:6–8). Too often, Christians blame God for their misery in a mixed marriage, even though he is not at fault.

Set Your Direction

Commit yourself to grow in your relationship with Christ and follow him, even if this commitment means conflict with your spouse. A clear stand on your priorities is important for your own spiritual health and for your witness to your spouse.[1] Compromise in the spiritual area is ineffective in winning a non-Christian spouse. (This is especially so when compromise goes to the point of sinful negligence, such as agreeing to leave Christian fellowship.) In our experience, virtually all unequally yoked Christians who won their spouse to Christ did so by first returning themselves to a strong commitment to Christ. It makes sense that few non-Christians would feel inclined to convert to a faith that carries little weight with their Christian spouse.

Show and Tell Your Faith

Be sure to live out your faith both in words and actions. Good behavior by itself will rarely win a non-Christian spouse, except in cases where a couple was already married when one came to the Lord. In cases where the Christian was converted *before* the marriage, good behavior may be interpreted as nothing new, or at least as nothing distinctively Christian.

Likewise, many Christians damage their witness because

97

they willingly preach what they believe, but their lives are so offensive their spouses are unlikely to listen. Christians who are demanding, demeaning, uncooperative, harsh, and selfish can rarely win their spouses through words alone.

Take inventory of your witness to your spouse. Do you need to talk less and do more? (See 1 Peter 3:1–2.) Or do you need to speak up more about spiritual issues? God says that both aspects of our witness—words and actions—are equally important and necessary.

> Compromise in the spiritual area is ineffective in winning a non-Christian spouse.

Get Help

Build solid relationships with other Christians. They are crucial in providing you with the spiritual support you need. Ask them to regularly pray for your spouse, and to pray that you will be an effective witness. Consider introducing your spouse to your Christian friends. When your spouse knows them, he or she will be less likely to feel threatened. Of course there are some Christian friends who might do more harm than good. But, generally, your Christian friends will find opportunities to share Christ with your spouse in ways that you cannot.

Be Careful With Children

If possible, you should seek to resolve any tensions arising out of a mixed marriage before having children. It's not always possible to save a mixed marriage, and Paul says that if the non-Christian spouse is unwilling to live with a Christian, he or she should be allowed to leave. (See 1 Corinthians 7:15.) If this were to happen, you would be better off without children. However, if you already have children, the decisions become more complicated, and you should talk to a good counselor or pastor.

Notes

1. In 1 Corinthians 7:14 (NIV) Paul says, "For the unbelieving husband has been sanctified through his wife, and the unbelieving wife has been sanctified through her believing husband." This promise probably means that the non-Christian spouse will receive added conviction from the Holy Spirit concerning his or her need for Christ. It does not mean they will necessarily be converted. (See v. 16.) This promise assumes that the believer is living out his or her faith. Paul never suggests that unequally yoked Christians agree to cease openly practicing their faith. If the non-Christian cannot handle living with a faithful, committed Christian, he or she may elect to leave the marriage. (See 1 Corinthians 7:15, NIV.) We believe that the statement "A believing man or woman is not bound in such circumstances; God has called us to live in peace" means the believer is not obligated to remain unmarried either.

EIGHT

SEXUAL LOVE OR EXPLOITATION?

The reproduction of mankind is a great marvel and mystery. Had God consulted me in the matter, I should have advised him to continue the generation of the species by fashioning them of clay.

—MARTIN LUTHER

As we saw earlier, the Bible has a very high view of human sexuality. Unlike many secular models, which view human sexuality as simply an instinctive, physical, procreative drive, the Bible teaches that sexuality is essentially connected to the deepest aspects of our personhood, made in the image of God.[1] God has designed sexual expression to be experienced between a man and woman within the context of a permanent love relationship. (See Genesis 2:24–25.) Christians who believe this should realize that sex will be fulfilling in a lasting way only in the context of marriage. If we pick a wildflower and take it from its natural environment, it wilts quickly. So, too, the satisfaction of sex is short-lived when it is torn from the setting for which God designed it.

Sex in Today's World

In today's world, sex has been removed from the category of moral behavior. Other than the lonely exceptions of rape and

101

incest, we no longer can speak in the modern West of sexual right and wrong. Instead we have only "sexual preference." Modern people believe they can violate God's design for sex without danger, as long as they practice "safe sex."

But immoral sex is *never* safe sex.

As modern people pursue their uninhibited sexual freedom apart from God's pattern, their families pay the price. Aside from the alarming rise in divorce discussed earlier, we see numerous other catastrophes descending on our culture that are directly connected to the rejection of sexual morals.

Consider, for example, the rise in illegitimate births. Children born outside of marriage have a dreadfully difficult time in life. On virtually every index of measurement, single-parent children are well below children from intact families.[2] Yet, because of permissive sexual attitudes and devaluation of the family, illegitimacy soars in spite of the fact that we perform millions of abortions! The following chart shows the rise in illegitimacy during recent decades.

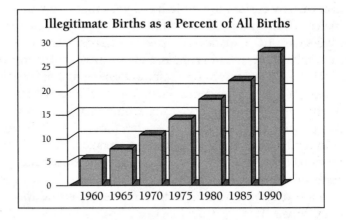

This chart portrays a shocking increase in the percentage of children born to unmarried women. Indeed, research shows that marriage is declining in all segments of the population at a stunning rate, while illegitimacy continues to rise.[3]

Most people are well aware of the increase in dangerous venereal diseases, including AIDS, so we won't cover that subject here. But have we realized that the spread of *internal, spiritual* damage from sexual immorality is just as real as the more visible spread of physical damage? In their lonely and driven lives, modern people are dragged, kicking and screaming, back to what they are: not mere organisms existing to seek maximum momentary pleasure, but sensitive creatures created in the image of God. Our inner fabric is like an exquisitely woven silk with a beautiful picture of ourselves in God's image. But like most objects of beauty, it tears when mistreated. We cannot disregard our personhood in the area of sexuality without tearing ourselves inwardly. These inner wounds are difficult but not impossible to overcome later in marriage.

Sexuality As God Intended

Are you excited about the possibility of enjoying sex with your Christian spouse? You should be. God is not against sex. He, after all, created sex and blessed it, not only after the Fall, but before it. (See Genesis 1:28.) But married sexuality will never conform to the standards of modern pornography. We are not here to ravish nameless physical shapes that can be discarded after our impersonal experience. Christian married couples who report satisfying sexual relationships always point to the same factors in this success: mutual trust and vulnerability, security based on a lifelong commitment, ongoing personal sharing, sexual self-control, and patience. The discovery of these couples should not be lost on us: To enjoy married sex, we have to nurture and build real, deep, and caring love through mutual understanding and self-sacrifice.

Contrary to our modern world's belief, our most important sex organ is neither our backsides nor our genitals. Our most important sex organ is located directly between our ears. Good sex begins and ends in our minds. Our expectations, our affections, and our perceptions are all dependent primarily on our inner lives with the Lord and with each other. One of the most damaging things many newlyweds bring into the bedroom is their own foolish and unrealistic expectations, often based on worldly erotic myths or their own past immorality. Modern people have not understood that successful sex does not come from having the perfect body and finding the dynamic sexual athlete who can perform up to our standards. Successful sex involves a successful human love relationship (and we're using love here in the Christian sense).

We should try to maximize our physical attractiveness, not as an egotistical discipline intended to bring attention to ourselves, but as a selfless act of giving for the benefit of our current or future mate. Our bodies are a stewardship. We should plan to show up on our marriage night with the most pleasant body possible for the sake of our spouse. We should continue to observe self-restraint after marriage, also for the sake of our spouse. We want to give our spouse the most pleasing gift possible when we take him or her into our arms. Although we don't want to fall into the modern trap of lavishing extraordinary attention on looking good and maintaining a movie star physique, it is right to do what

> Our most important sex organ is located directly between our ears.

we can to maintain our health and appearance, and to stay as attractive as we can. Being a Christian is not an excuse for presenting our spouse with a neglected body. (See 1 Corinthians 6:20.)

However, beyond this obvious point, have we also considered that something is even more important than enhancing our bodies? If we understand God's point of view, we realize that we need to protect our *minds* and our *spirits* in the sexual area. We need to protect our thinking so we can present ourselves in marriage as those who are substantially undamaged. We need to be able to enjoy loving our partner's body without holding him or her up to unrealistic and bizarre erotic images that fill our minds with lust. The biggest part of this mental preparation for marriage means carrying on our dating and engagement lives in a way that honors God and our partner.

Sex and Dating

All Christian dating couples experience sexual tension. The combined pressures of our culture and our own sex drives assure constant strong temptation in this area. At the same time, the Holy Spirit motivates and convicts Christians to maintain sexual purity. The resulting tension can produce profound suffering for serious single Christians. Many lower their personal standards of sexual conduct, believing that compromise won't hurt too much. But God holds forth high sexual ideals in Scripture, and he gives us solemn warnings of the consequences if we disregard his design.

Even within marriage, sex causes tension more often than not. For two people to come together in a lasting and successful sexual relationship is no small task. Differences in expectations, tastes, and appetites will automatically cause problems even in a marriage where the partners have laid a good foundation. Any problems we may have encountered in the past will make things even more difficult. We need every advantage we can get in the sexual area, and to get off on the right foot we should maintain strict sexual abstinence while dating.

In 1 Thessalonians 4:3–5, Paul says,

> This is the will of God, your sanctification; that is, that you abstain from sexual immorality; that each of you know how to possess his own vessel in sanctification and honor, not in lustful passion, like the Gentiles who do not know God.

Notice that Paul is not satisfied with a legalistic definition of sexual do's and don'ts. Beyond the obvious injunction against sexual intercourse outside of marriage, he condemns "lustful passion." Some who want to know exactly "how far they can go" in dating ask this question in honest ignorance. But others, in asking this question, betray a desire to go as far as they can without "crossing the line." Such a desire is legalistic and self-centered. The point is not to determine a legally defined "line," but to promote the emotional and spiritual well-being of both partners in the relationship.

105

Paul exhorts each of us to treat our own body and our partner's body with "sanctification and honor." (Although it is not always clear in the English translation, the term "his vessel" in this verse could refer either to "his own body" or to "his wife." See the NASB, marginal note.) We should respect God's design for our body's sexual expression. We are to give our body to our spouse only within the context of a permanent marriage commitment. (See Genesis 2:24.) Anything less than this dishonors the high purpose that God intends for our sexuality. Premarital sex is, therefore, self-centered—it seeks immediate physical pleasure at the expense of God's design for us and for our partner. It should be fairly obvious as well that those who practice premarital sex on an ongoing basis are also deliberately reserving the right to exit the relationship easily, should they decide to. In other words, when someone calls on you for premarital sex, he is really saying, "I want to use your body to satisfy my sexual appetite, but I want to remain free to reject you afterward."

> God isn't satisfied with a legalistic definition of sexual do's and don'ts.

The Importance of Premarital Purity

When we date seriously, or are engaged, we are trying to build a relationship suited to lifelong commitment to each other. We have to expend a great deal of effort learning to communicate deeply with each other, build healthy spiritual habits, and serve others as a team. Lack of sexual self-control will inhibit development in all of these areas. This is one of the worst consequences of immoral sex: At the very time we most need personal and spiritual development, our loss of self-control blocks our progress.

If we fail in the area of sexual control, how should we respond? Is it reasonable to expect that after an hour-long erotic session we will be able to comfortably finish the evening with prayer? We have difficulty praying and thanking God when our actions have just shown disregard for his will. Yet prayer is exactly what we need: not one of thanksgiving, but of repentance.

All Christians feel guilty after an experience of this kind, but there may be very little spiritual value in such feelings. The Bible does not command us to feel bad when we sin (like Judas did), but to change our minds. This may involve sorrow, but more importantly, it results in a change of action. Paul says, ". . . the sorrow that is according to the will of God produces a repentance without regret . . . but the sorrow of the world produces death" (2 Corinthians 7:10). In other words, sorrow could be good or bad depending on whether it leads to "repentance"—a change of heart. Until this change of heart takes place, we will continue to experience the alienation that results from knowing we have compromised in our commitment to God's will.

If, instead, we submit to defeat in our sexual lives, we will adversely affect our entire spiritual lives, begin to feel ill-at-ease around other growing Christians, and tend to withdraw from the body of Christ at the very time we need it most. We also fill our minds with erotic images that become the comparison point in our future sex lives.

> During episodes of immorality we fill our minds with erotic images that become the comparison point in our future sex lives.

Though our partner in an immoral episode may leave our lives, the images continue. These images are so powerful and enduring that we should exert every energy to avoid ever acquiring them in the first place. C. S. Lewis wisely wrote in his *Screwtape Letters*, "The truth is that wherever a man lies with a woman, there, whether they like it or not, a transcendental relation is set up between them which must be eternally enjoyed or eternally endured."[4]

Avoiding Defeat

When Jesus teaches us to pray "lead us not into temptation" (Matthew 6:13), he is reminding us that we need to handle the powerful drives of our physical bodies with care. Some Christians seem to have no respect for the power of their sex drives or of their sin-natures. They allow themselves to fall into late-night situations in empty houses or apartments, where it is unreasonable to expect sexual control. Some actually sleep together. But we cannot expect God's protection from sexual defeat if we climb into bed (or a couch or a sleeping bag) with our partners. This kind of practice is also hurtful to our Christian witness and to our example to other Christians. First Thessalonians 5:22 adjures us to "abstain from every appearance of evil."

The place to control sexual temptation is *before* we enter an uncontrollable situation. Together, dating couples should discuss the area of self-control and agree on standards and measures they will take to avoid temptation. For instance, going on dates with other people goes a long way in preventing immorality. Likewise, couples should agree to avoid those situations where they experience excessive temptation.

We might wonder whether these suggestions amount to controlling sin in an external, or superficial, way by controlling our outward circumstances. Shouldn't we simply avoid sexual misbehavior by drawing closer to God? Aren't we washing the outside of the cup (as the Pharisees did) by concerning ourselves with externals—such as where to spend our time while dating?

Although these questions make sense, they are naive. Sex is not a normal area of temptation. We all lust at times for money, and God wants us to learn to control that lust without dropping out of the working world. However, he does not take that view when it comes to fornication. With most sin, God says we should "stand firm against the schemes of the devil" (Ephesians 6:11). But when it comes to sex, he says "Flee fornication" (1 Corinthians 6:18, KJV). This flame is too dangerous and powerful to stand near! Even the most mature Christians can be tempted beyond their ability to resist if they allow themselves to be in the wrong situation. When sexual temptation flares up, it's time for the serious Christian to flee.

A Difficult Decision

If sexual problems persist in our dating relationships, we are faced with difficult decisions. We dare not simply carry on hoping for improvement when we know very well nothing will change. One godly option would be to break up until we gain more maturity. We may have to accept that it is better to lose a romantic relationship (perhaps temporarily) for the sake of sexual integrity than to compound our problems through premature marriage.

Sometimes Christian couples get married for no better reason than guilt feelings stemming from chronic sexual sin. But should guilt feelings be the basis for such an important decision? We think not. In fact, only when we are free from guilt feelings can we see clearly enough to decide wisely. Some Christians argue that to quit dating because of sexual defeat is a cop-out—just running from the problem. In fact, often the easy way is to remain in a relationship, even though it is causing both partners spiritual defeat.

To enter marriage with unresolved sexual problems may build an atmosphere of tension around the area of sex that often leads to sex-related problems in marriage. These problems vary widely from guilt or resentment toward each other, to suspicion of infidelity during times of stress, to problems with sexual responsiveness. For all these reasons, temporary or indefinite termination of the relationship remains a valid option for those struggling with sexual defeat in dating. Such a decision to sacrifice what we want in order to follow God's will is often a key step in spiritual growth. It is "[entrusting our] souls to a faithful Creator in doing what is right" (1 Peter 4:19).

Another option is to accelerate plans for marriage. This is a legitimate application of Paul's statement that ". . . if they do not have self-control, let them marry; for it is better to marry than to burn" (1 Corinthians 7:9). Certainly, Christians need to remember that marriage is God's provision for sexuality. On the other hand, much more than sexuality is involved in marriage, as we have seen. Therefore, any general rule that those who are having uncontrolled sexual desire should marry is wrongheaded. At the very least, a couple who marries mainly because of failure in their sex lives is entering marriage in a spiritually weakened state. Those who have recently suffered a striking defeat in such a central area will have problems. This is why some Christian leaders believe that sexual failure is reason to break up rather than to be married.

Who should opt for accelerated marriage in this situation? Essentially, those who are mature in the various areas needed in a successful marriage should consider moving ahead sooner than planned. Clearly, this is a subjective judgment rather than an objective one. There is no clear dividing line between those who should and those who should not move ahead into marriage. Some people clearly possess most of the needed elements for success, while for others, it is equally clear that because of their immaturity they will likely fail at marriage. For others still, there may be only a hazy balance between the dangers involved in marriage and the benefits.

Since such a decision must be determined on the basis of subjective judgment, only the couple involved can make the call, assuming they are adults. They, after all, are the ones who will have to live with the consequences of the decision. No one can spell out exactly how such a decision should be made, but the following guidelines should help.

Young or Old?

The chronologically young (i.e., teenagers or early twenties) should think about breaking up rather than accelerating marriage plans. Youthful marriages are known to fail more often than not.[5]

New or Mature Christian?

The spiritually young should also think about retreating rather than advancing toward marriage. An exception to this might be a situation where a couple has been living together before coming to Christ. In some cases they may elect to view themselves as already committed, and therefore seal their commitment by getting married.

Short Relationship or Long?

Those dating couples experiencing sexual defeat very early on should consider ending their relationship. On the other hand, if a couple has had a good record in this area during their dating relationship but is now struggling during engagement, it is often best to proceed with marriage. Because sexual temptation can be the most intense during engagement, consider the wisdom of a short engagement.

Christian Counsel?

Other Christians cannot and should not make this decision for you, as should be obvious from the fact that no two counselors will agree on the matter. But more mature Christians—especially those who know you well—may offer helpful insight. Their counsel should be prayerfully considered.

No matter how you decide the marriage question, you should reject any thought that getting married will solve the problems in your relationship, or in your life in general. Self-deception is common in this sort of decision, so consider what your natural bias would be: Do you tend to run away from difficult situations or barge ahead impulsively? Ask God to show you which direction is best.

Sexual Problems in Marriage

Some readers are already married and are finding the area of sex to be a serious problem in their relationship. (We will discuss this topic in more detail in Chapter 10.)

But first, remember that God changes lives. Resist any sense of fatalism in your sex life. Instead, as a first step, do some reading on sexual problems in marriage. A good source here would be John Gottman, *A Couple's Guide to Communication* (Champaign, Ill.: Research Press, 1976). If you can't find answers through reading, marriage counseling may be helpful to you in this area. The sooner you overcome your feelings of guilt and shame and are willing to seek help from a counselor, the better. If you delay too long, you may build patterns of behavior and attitude that can be very difficult (but not impossible) to change.

In most cases, developing a well-adjusted and mutually satisfying sexual relationship requires a number of years. Women often do not develop maximum sexual responsiveness until their late twenties. Couples should aim for a quality sexual relationship five to ten years into the marriage.

Although this is not primarily a marriage sex manual, we offer here three practical points that have given couples incredible mileage in their married sex lives:

1. *Sexual desire flourishes under positives, and perishes under punishment.* When expectations are not met, married people find it natural and easy to complain to their spouse. But sexuality is a hypersensitive area. It's easy to suggest our spouse change her hairstyle or that he wear a different style shoe. But when we complain about sexual performance, we strike at the heart of a person's identity and deep insecurity. Tread lightly with criticism in this area. A wise spouse realizes that glowing praise and appreciation accomplishes a hundred times more than criticism.

2. *The "demander" must become a responder.* What are the chances that two people with different body chemistries, different personalities, different genders, and different backgrounds will just happen to have the exact same appetite for sex? In fact, this rarely happens. When we read that married couples typically engage in sex 2.5 times per week, this doesn't mean they both wanted sex that often. It usually means one of them wanted it once every other week, and the other wanted it four times a week!

Sexual refusal can easily become a crack in the marriage that the Evil One seeks to widen into a gulf. Usually, in such situations, one partner tends to play the role of the "demander" and the other the "resister." Both need to learn how to resist their habitual tendencies.

Suppose a man is struggling with loss of sexual interest in his wife. The confusion and inner turmoil he feels at this time is matched only by his wife's feelings. For her to burst out in tears and suggest that he "doesn't love me anymore" is perhaps the worst thing she could possibly do to promote sexual functionality. Unfortunately, it's also probably the most common response. Such a complaint adds pressure and can literally crush any lingering responsiveness. Instead, she should learn patience, and how to show pleasure when he is interested. While waiting, she can ponder what other things she can do to make his sexual arousal more likely. The last thing a spouse who wants more sex in the marriage should do is to demand it.

3. *The "resister" must become an initiator.* Suppose it's the wife who finds her husband's frequent advances annoying or even dreadful. A routine of advance and refusal begins to take hold of the marriage, dictating roles that become entrenched. The wife who typically resists sexual frequency must fight an inner battle together with the help of God. She must learn to see that her husband's advances are not dirty or oversexed. But this isn't enough. She needs to become the one who makes advances. She needs to learn where her own sexual responsiveness lies, and focus on thoughts and images that stir interest. She needs to focus on bringing pleasure to her husband.

By negotiation, they need to agree that he will decrease his advances, and she needs to show that she will not take advantage of this freedom but will take up her own sexual role with zeal. For once, she needs to be the one trying to seduce her husband. As both partners act out roles different than their usual dysfunctional ones, they have an opportunity to break out of the cycle of despair that grips so many marriages. Hopefully, if she succeeds in playing a positive role, her husband won't miss his opportunity to make her feel appreciated and special. God

113

forbid that he should say, "That's more like it!"

Married couples may face many different challenges in the sexual area, including some we will discuss in later chapters. This is only one of the most common.

Many couples report good results from marriage seminars and retreats, such as Marriage Encounter. One of these may be a good idea whether you're feeling stumped, or just want to enhance your relationship.

Notes

1. Genesis 1:26–28 links man being made in the image of God with his sexuality and its expression. Since God is not physical and does not procreate, man's sexuality does not mirror God's essence in this way. Rather, this text and the subsequent discussion of sex in Genesis 2:18–25 suggest that humankind's sexuality within marriage is a reflection of the profound level of relational union between the Persons of the Godhead. God is One, but exists in a community of love relationships. People have the unique capacity to mirror that unity and diversity in the marriage relationship. Thus, our sexuality is an essential aspect of our identity and personhood.
2. This list could fill pages, and the research is all pointing the same direction—high risk for children in single-parent households. Here are a few examples: High school dropout rate higher for single-parent kids: Ralph B. McNeal, Jr., "Extracurricular Activities and High School Dropouts," *Sociology of Education*, Vol. 68 (1995), pp. 62–81. Deeper poverty for single-parent children: Leif Jensen, David J. Eggebeen, and Daniel T. Lichter, "Child Poverty and the Ameliorative Effects of Public Assistance," *Social Science Quarterly*, Vol. 74 (1993), pp. 542–559. More likely to have emotional and behavioral problems, more likely to drop out of high school, more likely to become pregnant as teenagers, to abuse drugs, and become delinquents: The National Center for Health Statistics, *Survey on Child Health* (1988), cited in William J. Bennett, *The Index of Leading Cultural Indicators* (New York: Touchstone Books, 1994), p. 52.
3. In a thirty-year study of marriage statistics completed at the University

of Wisconsin in 1991, the researchers reported "drastic decreases in marriage rates during the past 30 years," especially among blacks. Whites are following fast. See Mare and Winship, "Socioeconomic Change and the Decline of Marriage for Blacks and Whites," *The Urban Underclass*, Jenks and Petersen, eds. (Washington, D.C.: The Brookings Institute, 1991), pp. 175–196. The curve for growth of women between 24 and 29 who were never married was approximately the same as that for illegitimacy.

4. C. S. Lewis, *The Screwtape Letters* (West Chicago, Ill.: Lord and King Associates, Inc., 1976), p. 91.

5. The maximum frequency of divorce occurs between ages 24–27, and the median duration of marriage before divorce is 6.5 years. A moment's reflection reveals that the highest frequency of divorce occurs among youthful marriages. Alexander A. Plateris, *Duration of Marriage Before Divorce: United States* (Hyattsville, Md.: U.S. Department of Health and Human Services, Public Health Service, Office of Health Research, Statistics, and Technology, 1981), p. 1.

NINE

ARE WE MOVING IN THE SAME DIRECTION?

A man who marries a woman to educate her falls into the same fallacy as the woman who marries a man to reform him.

—ELBERT HUBBARD

A successful marriage is an edifice that must be rebuilt every day.

—ANDRÉ MAUROIS

We have already addressed most of the biggest questions about values and direction for those contemplating marriage. Our involvement in building deep relationships, learning to practice Christian maturity, self-control in our sexuality, and spiritual sharing while dating are usually good indicators of where our priorities lie. In fact, Christians often profess one set of priorities, but their lifestyles proclaim a different set. There is no substitute for objective progress reflected in action. If we ignore the facts, we will likely pay a high price for our negligence.

In addition to general values, such as spiritual growth and authentic belief in Christ, wise Christians will seek to marry those who share the same or compatible priorities and direction in life, even in certain less important areas. These areas don't measure up to the central values we have discussed so far, but

117

some of them could prove more important than we think in the intimate confines of marriage.

Marital Closeness Under God's Authority

When two people join their lives together, how do they decide on direction? What if one has habits or tastes that annoy the other? What if their priorities are different? In a secular marriage, there is no clear answer to these questions. Generally, counselors suggest couples should compromise or take turns in decision making. But these solutions don't always work. Spouses wind up saying, "We decided your way last time," and we open a new source of conflict. Similarly, consider how you would feel in this scenario: "We decided my way about which movie to see last night, but now we have to decide your way on which house to buy!"

Both trading off and compromising may be useful in some situations but are often problematic. Some decisions won't allow for compromise. Suppose a husband and wife don't agree in which area of town to live. If they compromise, they may end up living in an area they both hate. This is why in real life we find that the more powerful partner usually compels the weaker to comply with his or her agenda. Powerless partners have to decide how much they are prepared to take. The choice seems to be either slavery, perpetual power struggles, or flight. In cases where neither spouse is clearly more powerful, couples may engage in constant wrangling over even the smallest things.

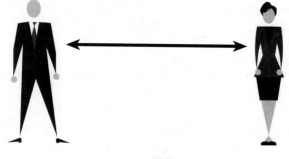

With Christ, we have an alternative way of life. We are no longer two people trying to get our own way. In a Christian relationship, both partners are concerned with discovering and following God's way.

Here is a basis for closeness. When other people's actions hurt or annoy us, what can we do? When we simply can't get someone close to us to be reasonable, where do we turn? We either try to make them change through force or manipulation, or we learn to keep our distance. No wonder modern people have trouble attaining intimacy in relationship!

But in a Christian relationship both partners have a starting point for closeness. On one hand, we have a reason for calling on the other person to change based on the will of God. On the other hand, we have an obligation to be willing to change ourselves in accordance with the will of God. Although we could still disagree about what God wants at times, at least we have some basis for agreement other than who has the most power. Finally, in Christ, we also have a basis for grace in relationships, which means we can forgive negatives in our spouse.

The paradigm of Christian couples living under the authority of God includes benefits and sacrifices for both partners. Most of the sacrifices are in the area of ego and selfishness. The

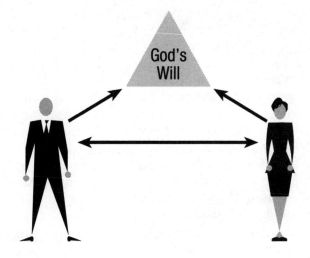

benefits are in the areas of closeness, the gratification of being used by God, and the joy of loving deeply.

Marriage Roles and Gender

In addition to the general idea of basing a marriage on the will of God, Scripture teaches that the husband should be the spiritual "head" in marriage. What does this mean? Headship is a troubling concept in our day, and we need to understand it in context.

Being the "head" in the biblical sense means the husband is responsible to *initiate love and self-sacrifice* for the well-being of his wife. (See Ephesians 5:22–29.) It does not mean the husband must be spiritually older than his wife, nor does it give the husband a license to insist on his own way. He is only to inquire of God's way.

Faithful exegesis of the relevant passages will show that God affirms male leadership in the home. Remember, however, that leadership in the biblical context is *servant leadership*. Paul said husbands should "love your wives, just as Christ loved the church and gave himself up for her" (Ephesians 5:25, NIV). This is the kind of leadership Christ demonstrated when he let himself be nailed on a cross for us. Jesus could be very authoritative, but he did not selfishly boss people around. He said, ". . . even the Son of Man did not come to be served, but to serve, and to give his life as a ransom for many" (Mark 10:45, NIV). When Jesus gives us a directive, it is not because he enjoys controlling us, but because he is concerned for our welfare. He also extends an amazing level of freedom to his followers, allowing us to defy his will and still continue our relationship without rejection. He will discipline us for our good, but he will never reject us. (See Hebrews 13:5.)

Coming under such self-denying leadership poses no threat to our happiness. A woman who submits to the servant leadership of a mature Christian man should be anticipating a life where her husband devotes himself to providing for her needs, protecting her, and, yes, directing her at times. A servant leader

120

will not insist on his way in areas where it is not possible to know objectively what God wants. He will call for his wife to follow Christ along with himself but will often graciously allow her to refuse his suggestions. Like Jesus, he will not compel obedience but will seek to win it through persuasion and love. The Lord doesn't force us to follow him; he wants us to follow willingly.

Any man (or woman) who is eager to assume such a role of leadership has probably not grasped what the Lord is saying in this passage. To be responsible for initiating love—for initiating self-giving—is a daunting role. Properly understood, no husband would object if his wife offered to lead the way in self-sacrifice for a while. The role of headship in a marriage is not a role of privilege, but of responsibility and self-sacrifice.

Our modern aversion to authority is incompatible with Christianity, not only because it flies in the face of biblical teaching, but because it is based on our fear of corrupt and self-serving authority figures.

Servant Leadership in Action

A Christian man should be spiritually mature enough to secure his wife's respect and basic willingness to follow his leadership, contingent, of course, on the higher authority of God.[1] When the Bible refers to wives submitting to their husbands, it essentially means wives should cultivate an attitude of respect for their husbands. (Note that in summing up the spouses' respective roles in Ephesians 5:33, Paul uses the word "respect" to describe the wife's role.) "Respect" in this context includes recognition of her husband as a legitimate leader—an inclination to go along with her husband's direction when possible. A wife who submits to her husband is free to suggest directions or to question and challenge

> The role of headship in a marriage is not a role of privilege, but of responsibility and self-sacrifice.

his direction. She is obligated to point out when she believes he is violating God's will. But she will turn away from self-willed resistance or manipulation.

Headship does *not* mean that only wives should be willing to defer to their spouses. In fact, willingness to defer to others for Christ's sake is the foundation of *all* relationships in the body of Christ. The verb "submit" in Ephesians 5:22 is really borrowed from verse 21: "Submit to *one another* in the fear of (out of respect for) Christ, wives to your husbands as to the Lord." Therefore, the wife's submission to the husband within Christian marriage is grounded in *both* spouses' willingness to defer to each other in love, as well as to other Christian friends in their church.[2] We are all to submit to Christ's moral leadership whenever it is expressed through others.

> Like Christ, the Christian husband is to lead the way in demonstrating a humble commitment to God's will rather than insisting on his own will.

All of this means we should emphatically reject the view that submissive wives let their husbands do all the thinking in the marriage, or must quietly ignore evil in their husband's lives. Neither does it mean that Christian husbands can be bossy and controlling. Biblical headship does not mean that the husband must decide on every matter pertaining to the household. Husbands and wives should negotiate and agree on who will take responsibility for paying the bills, grocery shopping, car maintenance, and other like matters. Creative and critical discussion between spouses about major decisions is *also* fully compatible with the idea of headship. Such discussion is necessary for a healthy marriage. If both spouses are committed to God and to the good of the other, most decisions can and should be mutual, and only the weakest husband would fear such discussions. In the rare cases in which husband and wife cannot agree on an important decision, the husband who has proven himself as a servant leader will usually be able to make a mature decision—either to hold to his view if necessary, or to sacrificially let his wife have her way, especially if no moral issue is involved.

Jesus' authority was valid because he did not seek his own will but the will of him who sent him (John 5:30). He also explained that he was willing to "lay down his life for the sheep" (John 10:15). In the same way, the Christian husband is to lead the way in demonstrating a humble commitment to God's will rather than insisting on his own will. He should take the initiative in practicing sacrificial service to meet his wife's needs, even at his own personal expense. Such husbands are usually able to secure their wife's trust and respect.

Both partners in a marriage should understand and agree on their concept of headship *before* getting married. Christians differ on how they interpret these passages, but however a couple understands them, they need agreement. Those already married may also need to rethink this area. If you are a married woman, are you comfortable responding to the spiritual leadership of your husband? Or is the idea of following your husband unrealistic or distasteful? Recognizing leadership in the home may be especially difficult for women who have experienced evil male authority figures, or who have adopted an ideology that opposes the concept of gender roles.[3] At other times, the husband's way of life makes it difficult for the wife to take his leadership seriously.

Whatever the causes, resolving these issues is important for Christian marriage. Additional reading on the subject of headship may help.[4]

Areas of Potential Conflict

The old adage says "love is blind." This adage means romantic lovers often fail to recognize shortcomings and areas of disagreement with their partners. Later, when the couple sets about establishing a household and building a marriage, these shortcomings and disagreements surface. When a couple is unskilled in problem solving, this can produce serious conflict and even threaten the marriage. To avoid such a situation, couples should think through possible problem areas before marriage.

Family Ties

What degree of independence from parents is appropriate? The Bible says men and women should "leave and cleave." This means the nuclear family based on marriage is to take precedence over earlier allegiance to parents. As a couple, you should decide, for example, how many visits you plan to make to out-of-town in-laws per year. Decide that you will respect the counsel of parents but reach your own decisions independently. Decide how you will handle excessive parental meddling.

Relationships With Future In-laws

Are the in-laws supportive of your marriage? If not, see the discussion of this subject in Chapter 10. Have you both been able to establish cordial relationships with your corresponding in-laws? If not, how will you deal with this in the future? A surprising number of serious conflicts arise in marriages in which the partners have not clearly communicated in this area.

Household

Do you both agree on what kind of house and neighborhood you will live in? Expectations about such things are often learned in childhood and accepted uncritically. Have these expectations been scrutinized according to biblical teaching on stewardship and materialism? How will each of your callings in ministry affect your living situation?

Previous Marriages

Have either of you been widowed or divorced? If so, have you frankly discussed these previous marriages? Are both of you confident that your previous marriages have been resolved so that they will not hinder your present marriage? (See Chapter 10.)

Jobs and Career

Have you both agreed that spiritual growth and serving God should take priority over career advancement? Are both of you willing to live more simply if need be in order to maintain this priority? Chapter 11 offers more guidance in the area of materialism.

If one of you is seriously committed to a vocational Christian ministry, are you both in genuine agreement with the pursuit of this goal?

Finances

Are both of you aware of *all* debts being brought into your marriage? Have you agreed on who will be responsible for paying bills, balancing checkbooks, and other financial matters? You should also seek agreement on major expenditures.

Sexuality

Have all previous sexual relationships or related problems been honestly discussed? Have you both done reading on this subject?[5] It is often wise for each of you to talk with a mature married person of the same sex shortly before your marriage.

Family Planning

You should agree before marriage on whether or not you want children. Be aware, however, that your views on this may change. If there are strongly divergent opinions you can anticipate problems. For instance, when a spouse is adamant about having no children it cannot be assumed that he or she will change his or her mind later on. Discuss how long you will wait before beginning to try to have children. If there are children from previous marriages, have you agreed on how they are to be raised?

Health

Do either of you have any serious illnesses or probable illnesses? If so, is the other person fully aware of it and the implications it may have for married life? Are there serious disagreements with each other's health habits (smoking, drinking, eating, exercise, etc.)? If so, how will you resolve these disagreements?

Personal Habits

Do either of you have any hobbies or habits that are time-intensive, potentially dangerous, or extremely repugnant to the other person? Have you discussed the possible adjustments that may need to be made in this area once you enter married life?

Resolving Differences

If you discover serious differences in any of these areas, you should work out a resolution. If you are unable to do so, especially in areas that could be critically important for marriage stability, you should seek counsel from more mature Christians, or consider waiting until you are able to reconcile your differences.

Many Christian couples discover these areas of disagreement only *after* they are married. When this is the case, open and honest discussion is very important. Both spouses should demonstrate a sincere willingness to see the other person's point of view and to modify their expectations in these areas. If serious disagreement remains, seek help from a pastor, a mature Christian friend, or a Christian marriage counselor.

In conclusion, take a sober estimation of your spiritual, emotional, and functional maturity before entering into marriage.

The more maturity you attain beforehand in these areas, the more effective you will be in building a lasting and stable marriage.

Notes

1. A Christian wife should never follow morally wrong directives from her husband. The principle of contingent, or conditional, obedience is well understood when it comes to secular authorities as in Daniel 2:1–18; Acts 4:19–20; and 5:29. Strangely, however, some commentators argue that wives should obey their husbands in an uncontingent and unqualified way! The text often used to justify this position is 1 Peter 3:5–6, which refers—with approval—to Sarah's obedience to Abraham when he lied to Pharaoh by saying Sarah was his sister. Based on this passage, some argue that even when Sarah complied with this situation, and nearly had to commit adultery as a result, she was doing the right thing. However, the passage does not condone this incident but only commends her attitude. In fact, God will hold individuals responsible for the wrong they do, even if they were ordered to do it, as the incident in Acts 4:19–20 demonstrates. Notice also that the circumstance to which 1 Peter 3 refers involves a sin of omission, not one of commission. The statement in verse 1 that wives should obey husbands, even if they are disobedient to the faith, means that the *husband himself* is disobedient, not that his directives are morally wrong.
2. The New American Standard Bible has chosen to indicate not only a new sentence in verse 22, but a new paragraph. This is in spite of the fact that verse 22 is a dependent clause sharing the participle "submitting" of verse 21. *The New American Standard Bible*, Referenced Version (Lockman Foundation, 1963), p. 300. See correctly the paragraph division in *New International Version of the New Testament* (Grand Rapids: Zondervan Bible Publishers, 1973). However, in our opinion, they still fail to bring home sufficiently the force of the shared action. (Later NIV editions have reverted to the traditional, wrong paragraph divisions.)
3. Feminist scholars have demonstrated that exploitation of women is a dominant theme in church history. However, to respond by holding that submission to anyone is a betrayal of one's own personhood is throwing out the baby with the bath water. Just because some have

abused the concept of male leadership in the home doesn't mean there is no such thing as a sacrificial servant leader.

4. See, for example, Richard N. Longenecker, *New Testament Social Ethics for Today* (Grand Rapids: Eerdmans Publishing Co., 1984), pp. 70–93.

5. See Ed Wheat, *Intended for Pleasure* (Old Tappan, N.J.: Fleming H. Revell Co., 1981).

TEN

OVERCOMING OBSTACLES FROM THE PAST: RELATIONSHIPS

Marriage has different attractions for different people. Those who marry for love want something wonderful and they sometimes find it. The people who marry because they want to escape something usually don't.

—CARL RIBLEY, JR.

We live in a cause-and-effect world. This means that our past affects our present—both positively and negatively. As Christians, we have God's unconditional forgiveness and need never fear his rejection. But our acceptance with God does not remove our fallenness. We not only have a sin-nature that sets its desire against God's will (Galatians 5:17), we also have areas of our lives that have been seriously injured by wrong environment, wrong thinking, wrong choices, wrong actions, and wrong habits. Christians are all, to differing degrees, damaged goods. We arrive at the Cross with major areas of our lives messed up and in need of repair.

The extent of damage we suffer is different for different people. There is nothing fair about Satan's world-system where people are spiritually and emotionally torn limb from limb. Some of us had the fortune to come from well-adjusted families, or we met and followed Christ at a young enough age that we managed to escape the worst types of damage. Others of us have had to grow in the Lord for years just to regain a basic level of functionality.

God's healing process is gradual and spans our entire lives. We have to cooperate with him as he seeks to transform our thinking, our choices, our behavior, and our habits. The greater the damage we have sustained, the longer God will need to work on us to bring about substantial healing.

Is Marriage an "Escape Hatch"?

When we consider marriage, we need to evaluate our past problems and how they may affect our prospective marriage. Many Christians and non-Christians think that marriage is the perfect "escape hatch" from their past. Actually, marriage often multiplies the destructive impact of former problems.

For example, consider uncontrolled anger. Some who struggle in this area may never actually "blow up" at their dates or fiancés. This may lead both partners to conclude that the anger will not cause problems in marriage, even though it may still be causing problems in other non-romantic relationships. After they get married, they are discouraged to find that their outbursts of anger are alive and well. When married, those who cannot control their anger typically turn their fits of rage primarily toward their spouses, often causing alienation and hurt within the marriage. Clearly, we should learn as much self-control over our anger as possible *before* marriage. We may also need to explore the reasons for our rage episodes.

But anger is no different than other areas of damage in our lives. Unresolved problems from the past are rarely solved by marriage, but the marriage can be damaged by them.

"Love Is Blind"

Dating and engaged couples almost invariably overlook or minimize each other's problems. Serious character flaws often do not surface during the premarital relationship because this relationship is both highly *selective* and highly *rewarding*.

The relationship is selective because each partner's knowledge of the other person is filtered through the very powerful grid of romantic attraction. The result is usually an idealized picture of the other person that exaggerates their strengths and minimizes their weaknesses. A dating couple usually spends time together in very positive and stimulating situations (such as going out to dinner) rather than in mundane or negative situations that reveal character flaws (such as cleaning the garage). During their dates, both partners are trying their hardest to be on good behavior in order to move the relationship toward consummation. The result is obvious: The truth about each other rarely comes fully into view.

Premarital relationships are also usually highly and unrealistically rewarding. During this stage, each partner receives positive reinforcement so powerful that it overshadows any shortcomings in the other person. We may gain a faint glimpse of a personality problem in our partner, but it seems to be manageable. This accounts for the uncanny tendency for dating couples to view their relationship as relatively problem free, while the

> Why don't we hear many married couples commenting that their spouses have changed for the better since their dating days?

same people, after marriage, believe their spouses have changed. Why are there so few married couples who feel their spouse has turned out to be better than they thought? Why don't we hear married couples commenting that their spouses have changed for the better since their dating days? Truly, "love is blind."[1]

As couples move into marriage, the blindness of romantic love wears off and both are confronted with a more realistic picture of who they and their spouse really are. Old problems that seemed to have vanished during courtship reappear, often to the shock and dismay of the spouse. The stresses and tedium of living together create many more opportunities for conflict. Romantic attraction no longer has the power to compensate for our spouse's flaws. These factors account for the element of disillusionment that most married couples go through early in marriage. Whether very early on, or over a period of several years, married couples begin to feel disappointment.

What determines whether this dangerous disappointed stage continues and escalates, or is gradually replaced by the satisfaction of a more mature relationship? Many factors are involved, but one key factor is the need to gain a realistic knowledge of each other's problems as soon as possible, especially before marriage.

Clearly, perfection is neither possible nor necessary before we can have a successful marriage. We can also take comfort from the knowledge that with the power of God, even serious problems can be resolved within marriage. But a clear awareness of our major areas of damage, coupled with some experiential success in counteracting these areas, is a tremendous asset to take into marriage.

This chapter and the next one address typical major problem areas we may encounter. Not surprisingly, they correspond to those addressed by the apostles in their letters to Christians two thousand years ago. (For further study, see Ephesians 4:17–5:21; Colossians 3:5–17; 1 Thessalonians 4:1–12; Romans 13:8–14; 1 Corinthians 6:12–20; Philippians 2:1–16; James 1:19–21; 3:1–18; 4:1–17; 1 Peter 1:22–2:3; 3:8–9; 4:3; and 1 John 3:14–18.) Though cultures change, humankind's sins do not. This chapter focuses on relational problems; the next chapter focuses on ideological and addictive problems.

Sexual Damage

Our sexuality is not an unattached area of our lives that we can casually express without it affecting us. Rather, sexual experiences deeply impact our lives positively or negatively, de-

132

pending on whether we express our sexuality according to God's design. Sex has the capacity to increase our sense of security and joy. It also has the capacity to increase our loneliness and alienation when we express it promiscuously. Sex has the capacity to help us enjoy relational intimacy, but it also has the capacity to make us fear intimacy when we have been sexually abused. Sex has the capacity to make us feel good about our identity; it also has the capacity to profoundly confuse our identity when we express it with the wrong gender. If we have been affected in some way by sexual experience, we need to be aware of that fact and of how it may affect our marriage.

The following areas of sexual behavior all involve deviations from God's design. Since they do not conform to his intended pattern for sex, they are damaging to various degrees. We will only identify common problem areas and suggest general directions for solutions. Healing the damage from any of these areas could take years and may require professional help. While this is not a detailed study of sexual and relational healing, it should be helpful to identify areas that could cause problems. We will do best if we also gain a measure of healing in these areas before entering marriage. However, we can experience healing within marriage if we are committed to continued growth together.

Rape, Molestation, and Incest

Although these experiences are usually forced upon the victim, often at an early age, victims nonetheless commonly experience deep-seated guilt feelings and an abiding sense of shame. These, in turn, may produce chronic feelings of depression or anger. In the case of molestation or incest, there may be different results if the victim voluntarily continued sexual involvement following the initial incident. Promiscuity and dreadful temptations often afflict those who were induced to partake in juvenile and early teen sex. In other cases, especially those where the victim did not consent, frigidity and general aversion to sex is not unlikely.

Those who have unresolved hatred toward family members involved, or toward men in general (in the case of rape), need to take those feelings to the Cross and resolve them for their own sake. God will substantially heal these problems if we face them honestly and bring them to him. In most cases, we should take these problems into the confidence of a qualified Christian counselor.

If you are a sexual abuse victim considering marriage, you should definitely tell your future spouse what happened to you. Your disclosure need not go into all the humiliating details, but it should be specific enough to communicate the manner and duration of abuse. Such a disclosure will help to alleviate your fears of rejection and hasten fuller healing by enlisting your partner's help. Your honesty will also help your loved one be more sensitive in the sexual area of the relationship after marriage.

Over the last decade, many have rightfully exposed the extent to which sexual abuse occurs in our society. Compassionate Christians will grieve for those who have been damaged by this terrible abuse and betrayal. But along with compassion, we should also communicate confidence in Jesus Christ to substantially heal the effects of sexual abuse. Gwen's story is an example of someone whose life was transformed by the love of Christ.

> If we have been affected in some way by sexual experience, we need to be aware of that fact and of how it may affect our marriage.

Gwen, along with her sisters, was sexually abused by her stepfather from the time she was ten until she was fourteen. Not surprisingly, she experienced tremendous anger toward her stepfather and her mother, who willfully ignored the signals of the abuse. Gwen was also plagued by intense guilt feelings because she herself did not take greater measures to stop the abuse.

When she came to Christ at age sixteen, God convicted Gwen almost immediately of her need to forgive her stepfather. She did this, even though she had to reaffirm this decision many times as she experienced the ongoing effects of his abuse. She also followed God's leading to move away from home when she turned eighteen, despite her mother's pleas to stay. The next few years were deeply painful for Gwen. She agonized as her siblings continued to reap the effects of living in such a dysfunctional home. She struggled to trust God's authority over her life since she had been so horribly betrayed by her own parents. But despite her pain, she determined to make her life count for Christ. She developed a genuine heart for ministry as she worked with high school girls through a Christian evangelistic organization. Even though men flocked to her because she was so attractive, she committed herself to marry only someone who was likewise committed to serving Christ.

When she and her future husband, Bill, neared engagement, she told him about how she had been abused. He had no training in sexual abuse, and they had no access to Christian professional counseling. They often discussed and prayed about the hurtful issues as they emerged from Gwen's heart. They worked as a team to relate to Gwen's family in ways that expressed love and forgiveness but which firmly resisted their manipulation. Most important, they both remained committed to each other and to serving Christ together in the context of vital Christian fellowship.

Their relationship has had its ups and downs, but Bill and Gwen have now been married for almost two decades and have children of their own. Their home is a hub of ministry to young people, many of whom express gratitude for their example of a healthy Christian marriage. Not surprisingly, Gwen has been greatly used by God in helping other victims of sexual abuse. They are both amazed and encouraged to learn how God has transformed Gwen's life as she cooperated with God's healing process.

Heterosexual Promiscuity

In today's culture, many Christians have been sexually promiscuous during at least part of their lives. Whether you were promiscuous with many people over short periods of time, or with few over longer periods of time, problems often result. Unresolved promiscuity before marriage can cause sexual dissatisfaction within marriage, or inappropriate and harmful sexual habits and attitudes. For example, the habit of comparing the sexual qualities of one's spouse with others is both frustrating and damaging. No one can live up to all of the good qualities of several other past sexual partners, and no one should have to try to do so.

Promiscuity also unavoidably includes the selfish notion of sex as self-gratification at another's expense. This motivational base, however, is the antithesis of biblical sexuality, where sexual love is a way to give to our spouse. In sexual love, we savor and enjoy one another's bodies, secure in the knowledge that no matter what happens, we will remain committed and learn how to pleasure each other. When we view sex as something intended to give maximum pleasure to self, adultery becomes very likely. It's only a matter of time before a new sex opportunity will be able to deliver more pleasure than making love once again with our mate.

Our damaged and sub-biblical definitions of erotic love come in at this point to supply the rationale for immorality. New romances are often more exciting than old ones, and if our measure of marital happiness is based on intensity of erotic love, how long will it take before some new lover can deliver more thrill than our spouse?

We all are affected today by the *eros* myth. But those who have engaged in immorality face special pain and struggle in the area of *eros*-worship. We heap a devastating burden on our spouse when we will be satisfied with nothing less than present erotic desire equal to our past immoral episodes. No wonder sexual promiscuity is so intensely addictive!

God's pattern for marriage is that "the two become one"

(Genesis 2:24). In order to do this, other sexual experiences have no place in our marriage. We can expect sufficient resolution of any past sexual experiences to predict sexual adjustment in marriage. Our past is never forgotten, but we can experience a reshaping of our thought life in the sexual realm. How do we know whether we have changed enough in this area? Try asking yourself the following questions.

- Have you been able to maintain consistent chastity in your dating? If not, why do you think you will be able to control yourself when married?
- How long ago was your last promiscuous episode? Has there been sufficient time for healing?
- Are you gaining more self-control in turning away from acting on sexual lust? Are you able to turn away from conduct such as deliberate flirtation, titillation with others, suggestive conversations and actions, etc.?
- Is there evidence that your basic view of the opposite sex is healthy and biblical?

Single as well as married Christians may need to develop supportive relationships with members of the same sex who understand the problem of runaway sexual lust. When we talk about our sexual problems with Christian friends of the same sex *before* acting, temptation loses some of its power. Our same-sex friends are not personally hurt when they hear about our lustful impulses, as our future spouse might be. Those of us who are married and struggling with a certain chronic temptation should also seek help by confessing this to a same-sex friend. But if this doesn't free us from temptation's grip, we must also tell our spouse no matter how it makes them feel. Sexual obsession works in secret, and unveiling it is often the first step in gaining control. In the end, only long-term success at refusing sexual opportunities offers any assurance of victory.

Homosexuality

The Bible says homosexual activity is a sin just like other sins.[2] The Bible rejects the notion that homosexuality is a disease or a permanent character trait like eye color, even though genetic factors may contribute to homosexual tendencies. (See note at end of chapter.)

Just as heterosexuals have tendencies toward sin, some people may be tempted to commit homosexual sin. But this does not mean they cannot help sinning in those areas. We believe learning (including the person's choices) plays a very large part in the development of homosexual orientation—in fact, even a larger part than genetic predisposition. And since this is the case, Christians who have learned a homosexual way of life can gain true and lasting liberation from homosexual sin by choosing to follow Christ. This belief is not a theological abstraction; it is backed up by real-life examples.

Mike's earliest sexual experiences were exclusively with other boys. As far back as he can remember, he felt sexual attraction to men rather than women. After succumbing to homosexual temptation in high school, he spent several years living the gay lifestyle. When Mike came to Christ, he experienced the liberating and cleansing effect of God's forgiveness. In spite of his verbal defense of homosexuality, he had always believed it was morally wrong. Now he knew God's Word confirmed the witness of his own conscience.

He took a strong stand for sexual purity in his own life and began gradually to grow into a mature Christian. But he continued to wonder if he would ever be able to have a successful marriage. He still experienced sexual lust toward other men, but never toward women. How could he possibly entertain the idea of getting married unless he was first able to experience heterosexual arousal?

Mike and Jane got to know each other as they studied and ministered together in their home fellowship group. From the beginning, Jane was romantically attracted to Mike. Even more important, she respected his godly character. Mike likewise respected Jane for her commitment to Christ. He also prized their deepening friendship, but he felt no sexual attraction for her. At the appropriate time, Mike revealed his previous homosexual involvement and its continuing effects in his life. Jane was surprised and concerned—but she loved him and trusted God's changing power enough to continue their relationship. Based on reading that indicated sexual reorientation is possible, they began to move prayerfully toward marriage, trusting that, as they continued to build their relationship based on Christian love, God would grant Mike sufficient sexual healing.

Ten years later, Mike and Jane have a healthy and enjoyable marriage. Their children have enriched their relationship, and both are excellent parents. Mike still struggles occasionally with homosexual lust, but he has experienced substantial sexual reorientation within their marriage and has been totally faithful to his wife. They are both grateful beyond words for the privilege of serving Christ as husband and wife. Together, they have weathered the normal trials of married life in the same way they have handled Mike's homosexual damage—by rooting their thinking in scriptural truth and being committed to a lifestyle of sacrificial love.

Today, thousands of formerly homosexual and bisexual Christians like Mike have gained victory either through celibacy or sexual reorientation within marriage. We personally know numerous cases of success in reorientation. They are testimony to the fact that homosexuality is ultimately a behavioral issue, not a genetic one. Militant homosexuals argue that reoriented ex-homosexuals who continue to experience temptation are "just faking it." Nothing has really changed.

But Mike and others would not agree. This claim is no truer than the claim that formerly promiscuous people, who are tempted to heterosexual sin, are faking it when they resist temptation. People who have experienced episodes of sexual pleasure (including immoral pleasure) of any kind may very well struggle with temptations in that area for the rest of their lives. We need not plunge ourselves into ruin and despair by indulging the desires of our sin-nature. Sexual immorality is a great betrayer because it can never deliver a happy life, or even sexual satisfaction. It only delivers more desire.

Homosexuality is a very habit-forming way of life. The stimulation of immoral sexual thrills is so powerful it can temporarily dwarf normal sexual pleasure. But the pain and emptiness that come with immorality are also severe. Although it is difficult to break the homosexual habit, God has the power to change lives.

As with heterosexual promiscuity, those with homosexual or bisexual pasts should seek evidence that they have gained substantial victory before risking marriage. This can be difficult to assess since sexual reorientation rarely occurs outside of actual sexual contact, something that the Bible says should be reserved for *after* marriage. It may seem like an incredible risk to get married on the theory that the homosexual partner will successfully reorient when the time comes. But in fact, if the homosexually oriented partner demonstrates key signs of spiritual and emotional maturity, the risk is minimal. After all, previously promiscuous heterosexual couples also take a risk when they marry. How do we know heterosexuals with immoral pasts won't revert to their former way of life? Again, the key is spiritual and emotional maturity. We have witnessed remarkable success at homosexual reorientation when those involved in the marriage are mature. Some of these marriages have been tested for over a decade and show no sign of weakening. Scientific literature also bears this out.[3]

> Sexual immorality is a great betrayer because it can never deliver a happy life, or even sexual satisfaction—only more desire.

Those with any homosexual or bisexual history need to ask themselves questions like the following in order to determine whether they have made sufficient progress to risk marriage.

- Have you frankly shared the truth about the past with your present partner? He or she must know the risks and freely take them on with you.
- Have you been able to abstain completely from physical ho-

mosexual involvement long enough to assure that it will not be a problem in the future? Homosexual fantasies and desires will not necessarily disappear, but you can gain the ability to turn away from all sexual contacts, including homosexual pornography. An "adequate period of abstinence" should probably be assessed in terms of years rather than weeks or months.

- Have you gained self-control in the area of lesser homosexual-related actions? These include deliberate flirtation, titillation with others, visiting gay social locations, suggestive conversations and actions.
- Have you developed the ability to aggressively love and discipline others? The passive or fatalistic element in the lives of many gay men and lesbians should be countered with the biblical realization that we have a basis for confronting others in love. Direct confrontation should take the place of indirect punishing through sexual nonconformity.
- Have you demonstrated the ability to deal effectively with feelings of rejection from the same and opposite sex? Some homosexuals fear leaving the gay lifestyle because they perceive an increase in the danger of rejection. It takes real courage and faith in God to leave the "security" of a homosexual lifestyle for one where you might not be accepted as readily.
- Have you established a pattern of commitment in non-romantic relationships? Or do you move from friend to friend, never building very deeply? The homosexual lifestyle is usually diffuse. Deep friendships that last over the years are rare. For those leaving the gay lifestyle, any tendency to move from one friend to another is a serious warning sign. You, more than others, need to ensure that you have built friendships all the way to the intimate level in a non-sexual context.
- Are you able to relate to friends based on commitment without demanding a "love feeling" from them? Present love feelings, or stimulation, is the basis for the gay lifestyle. Marriage and sexual reorientation will not be possible unless you have developed a taste for committed, rather than stimulation-based, love.

- If you are male, have you developed the ability to perceive yourself as a male who is both aggressive *and* sensitively caring? Many gay males have difficulty integrating these two dimensions in the male gender.
- If you are female, have you resolved your ambiguous feelings toward men and masculinity? If you have a background including sexual abuse or rape, see the sections on those problems above.

Spouses of previously gay men or lesbians will need to exercise patience during a partner's sexual reorientation. The ex-homosexual may initially demonstrate a deficiency in sexual attraction or a timidity which may be frustrating. Only a patient and non-demanding demeanor will succeed in drawing out sexual interest. Plan on allowing a certain amount of time (often less than a year) for normal levels of sexual desire to develop. Couples planning a marriage involving sexual reorientation of one or both partners should usually work with a competent counselor or knowledgeable pastor. But make certain that any counselor or pastor you work with has not bought into the modern secular belief systems on this issue. The counselor must believe that sexual reorientation is possible and right.

Divorce

Any divorce poses a serious challenge to further marital success. Statistically, the divorce rate for marriages in which either or both partners have been divorced is almost double that for first-time marriages.[4] This is a very imposing statistic, because it means the vast majority of second attempts at marriage will fail. Those who have cohabited for some time also experience increased failure in marriage, as we have seen. Their statistics are similar to those who have been divorced. In the church it is not uncommon to see cases of second marriages that succeed, especially when the first marriage was in a non-Christian context. However, failures are also common, which suggests the need for caution.

Most pastors and counselors know all too well the reasons

for this high failure rate. In the first place, people usually learn little or nothing from a failed marriage. Divorcees usually blame their ex-spouses for the problems that led to divorce, with little understanding of the role they played in the failure. But marital problems are virtually never strictly the result of one partner's sin. Underlying the divorcees' blame perspective is the thought that if only they had married someone else, all would have been well. Such thinking is antithetical to our argument all along, which is that the key is not just to *find* the right person for marriage, but to *become* the right person for marriage. As long as divorcees remain unable to see where they (not their ex-spouses) went wrong, the chances of a repeat performance are likely.

Once divorcees gain some understanding of what was wrong with their *own* way of relating, the first brick is in place. But it's not enough. They still need to make progress in changing those patterns. Any hope that merely marrying a different spouse will correct the problem is usually forlorn.

> According to statistics, the vast majority of second attempts at marriage will fail.

Another reason for repeated failure is that divorcees tend to repeat their own bad choices of whom to marry. Divorcees often choose a new mate externally different than their ex-spouse, but beneath the externals, we can see the same criteria for choice at work.

Finally, in some cases it might not be ethical to remarry after a divorce, unless it is with the estranged spouse. Christians need to determine where they stand with regard to the ethical principles given in the Gospels and in 1 Corinthians 7 before moving into another marriage. There are several ways of understanding these passages, including ways that would permit remarriage after most divorce situations.[5]

These passages are written to normal lay believers, not just Bible experts. Therefore, you should be able to enter into a study of the passages with help from study aids and reach your own conclusions. You may also need to check with your church leaders on how they understand the passages, especially if you expect them to perform the marriage. Until both partners feel comfortable with the correctness of marriage in their situation based on a study of God's Word, they cannot go ahead with confidence.

Failed Past Romantic Relationships

Most adults date different people during the process of making their marriage choice. Especially during the teenage years, people typically go through a number of dating relationships. But when the pattern continues into adulthood, those failing often at serious relationships need to ask, Why did the relationships fail? Sometimes answers to this question point to personal problems that should be addressed.

Was it that you felt a strong attraction for someone that faded away later on? If so, this may indicate that you have an inappropriate understanding of love. If you regularly had such a problem, you may be interpreting relationships mainly in terms of erotic love, and this will probably lead to disappointment in marriage. You should work on developing a more stable and mature love capability as described in Chapters 3 and 4.

Sometimes Christians get involved with someone first, only to discover later that the person is fundamentally uncommitted or uninterested in spiritual things. When this happens regularly, it may indicate a faulty set of values when choosing whom to date.

Perhaps the partners in your deep relationships seem to want out after a while. This might be an indication that you relate in certain immature ways that are repelling others from closeness with you. It may not be a case of gross sins of commission such as verbal abuse. You may only be guilty of sins of omission. For instance, you may be overly dependent on other people to carry the burden of the relationship, or you may be perceived as boring because you are not initiating creatively.

If you have had problems with romantic relationships, is there evidence that the problems have been dealt with? What do your close friends think of your progress in practicing mature love? If you do not know their feelings, you should ask them for their criticism, with real willingness to hear their advice.

Family Damage

Sometimes, people view marriage as an escape from painful problems with parents. Such a view is unwise for at least two reasons.

First, being married will not eradicate problems with our parents. They will continue to play a role in our lives whether we are married or not. When we are bitter toward our parents, we continue to be adversely affected because our emotional focus is on the injury (real or imagined) we have incurred from them. The Bible teaches us to "leave father and mother" so that we may "cleave" to our spouse (Genesis 2:24). But when we are bitter, we are unable to break away from the negative emotional focus, and this brings a negative influence into the marriage. Forgiveness, not anger and withdrawal, is the way to become liberated from this kind of negative emotional focus. Couples should help each other resolve this kind of bitterness *before* marriage if possible.

Second, we have to learn to deal maturely with parental manipulation or other wrongful influence even after marriage. Marriage will not magically change this kind of parental behavior, especially when children enter the picture. The more we have learned to lovingly counter manipulation while unmarried, the easier it will be to do so in marriage. Couples should also help each other relate to their parents prior to marriage, so that as a couple they have already established loving, righteous ways of dealing with their extended families.

Most parents want what is best for their children, even though we may disagree with them on what "best" is. Because of their legitimate concern for our well-being, and because they know us so well, any caution or objection they offer to our marriage plans should be seriously considered. Open discussion of the reasons for their concern demonstrates both respect and wisdom. In many cases, their concern is valid and helpful in forging successful marriages.

Some people think parental permission is not only desirable but necessary before marriage can be considered within God's will. This position seems unwarranted. The passages used to argue this point are often addressed to *tekna* ("Children [*tekna*] obey your parents . . ." Ephesians 6:1). Surely, although young children should obey their parents, this passage probably is not teaching that we must obey our parents throughout our lives. Other passages merely call for us to show honor to parents. (See Exodus 20:12.) In any event, whatever obedience may be due to parents by adult Christians is not unconditional but contingent on other factors, as with all obedience to human authority. (Compare Romans 13:1 with Acts 5:29.) Some atheistic or Muslim parents, for example, would never consent to a Christian marriage. Gaining the approval of parents for marriage plans is a value that we should pursue but is not necessarily a prerequisite for marriage. A new couple will certainly benefit if they find a way to gain their parents' approval for marriage.

Notes

1. For a helpful discussion of this phenomenon, see Neil S. Jacobson and Gayla Margolin, *Marital Therapy: Strategies Based on Social Learning and Behavior Exchange Principles* (New York: Bruner/Mazel, 1979), pp. 21–22.
2. Homosexuality is not singled out as distinct from the rest of the sexual sins described in the Mosaic Law, although it takes its place as one of the serious sins (Leviticus 20:10–21). In Romans 1:24–32 it is named as

one of the serious results of fallen man's revolt against God. Paul lists homosexuality along with other moral problems in 1 Corinthians 6:9–10.

3. For an excellent treatment of this issue, see Stanley R. Strong, "Christian Counseling With Homosexuals," *Journal of Psychology and Theology* (1980), pp. 279–287.

4. "One of the most clear-cut findings from the 1970 divorce data is the high likelihood of divorce for persons who have been married more than once. . . ." *Divorces and Divorce Rates* (Hyattsville, Md.: U.S. Department of Health, Education and Welfare: Public Health Service, National Center for Health Statistics, 1980). Put differently, the average duration of marriage before divorce is only half as long for the second marriage and one-third as long for third marriages. *Duration of Marriage Before Divorce: United States*, (Hyattsville, Md.: U.S. Department of Health and Human Services: Public Health Service, Office of Health Research, Statistics, and Technology, National Center for Health Statistics, 1981), p. 12ff.

5. From a lenient point of view, see James M. Efird, *Marriage and Divorce: What the Bible Says* (Nashville: Abingdon Press, 1985). For a more technical survey of various views and of exegetical and linguistic issues, see Donald W. Shaner, *A Christian View of Divorce According to the New Testament* (Leiden, The Netherlands: E. J. Brill, 1969). For a mixed view, see John MacArthur, *The MacArthur New Testament Commentary: 1 Corinthians* (Chicago: Moody Press, 1984), pp. 153–186.

A Note on Homosexuality and Science

Scientific studies of various factors in the formation of homosexual orientation have not demonstrated a "gay gene" as some popular media have reported. On the other hand, some partial correlation has been demonstrated between genetic relatedness and likelihood of later homosexual orientation. "Genetic Study of Male Sexual Orientation," by Richard Pillard and Michael Baily, of Boston and Northwestern Universities respectively, published in the mid-eighties, reported that gay-gay concordance rates are 11% for nonrelated adoptive brothers. That is, if one adoptive brother is homosexual, the other brother will be homosexual about 11% of the time, even though they have no genes in common. For nonidentical twins and regular brothers, where only part of their genetic makeup is shared, this rate is around 22%. But for identical twins, who have the same genetic makeup, the rate is around 52%. In other words, identical twins are about twice as likely to exhibit gay-gay concordance as are fraternal twins. They are also five times as likely to exhibit concordance as adopted brothers who share an upbringing but no genes. See David Fernach, "Xq28 Marks the Spot," *New Statesman and Society*, Vol. 6 (July 30, 1995), p. 29; David Nimmons, "Sex and the Brain," *Discover*, Vol. 15 (March 1994), pp. 64–67.

These findings suggest that genetics play some role in homosexual orientation, but they also clearly *disprove* the notion of genetic determination: that gays are born that way. If genes determined sexual orientation, all identical twins would share the same sexual orientation, just as they share the same eye color—not just 52%. This is a very important distinction when it comes to ethics. We clearly would not assign moral blame for something that a person is born with. But this genetic tendency toward homosexual temptation leaves ample room for human choice and learning. Note also that these statistics are not for identical and fraternal twins raised in separate homes. Such identical twins provide a better control for separating genetic and environmental factors. These twins shared the same upbringing, and may even have influenced one another in some cases. Therefore, the actual genetic portion of cause for the concordance between these twins is likely a good deal lower than 50%. Before drawing ethical conclusions from this data, consider that scientists have demonstrated very similar rates of concordance for alcoholism and pedophilia. Yet, the same people who condemn pedophilia and call for longer prison sentences will turn around and insist that homosexuality is innate and completely beyond the individual's control.

Another problem with recent research on the "gay gene" and "the gay brain" is researcher bias. Dean Hamer's finding of a gay genetic factor at the tip of the X chromosome in 1993 was reported as the first molecular evidence that human sexual orientation might be determined genetically. See John Horgan, "Gay Genes, Revisited," *Scientific American* (November 1995), p. 26; Richard Norton, "Xq28 and the Brain Structures Tied to Sexuality," *The Lancet*, Vol. 346 (November 11, 1995), p. 1289; Joseph P. Shapiro, Traci Watson, "Is There a 'Gay Gene'?" *U.S. News and World Report*, Vol. 119 (November 13, 1995), p. 93.

However, since his research was released, Hamer has been criticized for it. The Office of Research Integrity (ORI) in the Department of Health and Human Services began an investigation after reports by one of his junior lab members that Hamer's methods of data selection were biased. According to the Chicago Tribune, which printed the story in June of 1995, the ORI was looking into allegations that Hamer "selectively reported his data." He was accused of "improperly excluding pairs of brothers whose genetic makeup contradicted his finding." See Elliot Marshall, "NIH's 'Gay Gene' Study Questioned," *Science*, Vol. 268 (June 1995), p. 1841.

A second attack on Hamer's research came in 1995, from neurogenetics researcher George Ebers. He reported that he had not been able to replicate Hamer's finding. At the University of Western Ontario in London, Ontario, Ebers collected data on 52 pairs of gay brothers, just as Hamer's did, but he found no evidence that gayness is passed on from mother to son—"not even a trend in favor of the X-linkage." Hamer responded to this by saying Ebers' "research design is very different than our own and cannot be interpreted to either refute or confirm our findings." See Marshall, "NIH's 'Gay Gene' Study Questioned," p. 1841.

Another critic has charged that Hamer "deliberately sought out an extremely unrepresentative sample." See Fernach, "Xq28 Marks the Spot," p. 29. In responding to these critics, Hamer said their results "cannot be extrapolated to individuals who do not meet our inclusion criteria. . . ." See Norton, "Xq28 and the Brain Structures Tied to Sexuality," p. 1289. He also admitted that some heterosexual brothers possess the suspect region, while some homosexual men do not. "This gene is not acting like some automatic switch that makes you one way or the other," he said. See John Travis, "X Chromosome Again Linked to Homosexuality," *Science News*, Vol. 148 (November 4, 1995), p. 295.

Research bias can be exaggerated by inaccurate media reporting of research. For example, neurobiologist Simon LeVay studied the third interstitial nucleus of the anterior hypothalamus, or INAH3, of heterosexual males and females and gay men. The INAH3 is a tiny cell cluster smaller than this letter "o" that accounts for .000009% of the brain's mass. The idea was that if a difference was found between a key sexual center of the brain of gay and straight men, "that would imply sexual orientation was influenced by—or at least reflected in—anatomy." This last phrase is important. How would we know whether differences in such a structure in the brain were the *cause* of homosexuality or the *result*? Perhaps it is neither, but a coincidental correlation arising from other environmental factors. Nevertheless, the media, including national network news, reported that this research demonstrated that gays are born that way.

Several other factors reduce further the significance of LeVay's findings. For one thing, the study was very small. He only autopsied the brains of 19 homosexual men and 16 heterosexual men. Also, some critics questioned whether the AIDS virus could have skewed the results, because all of the gay men died from AIDS. LeVay thought that was "highly unlikely." LeVay, who is reportedly homosexual, has been more fair in assessing his own work than has popular media. He admits that "I did not prove that homosexuality is genetic, or find a genetic cause for being gay. I didn't show that gay men are 'born that way,' the most common mistake people make in interpreting my work. Nor did I locate a gay center in the brain." He only looked at adult brains, which means we cannot draw conclusions about brain structure in babies or fetuses.

Even these limitations would lead to caution in impartial readers. But there is more. Anne Fausto-Sterling, a developmental geneticist at Brown University says, "He [LeVay] claimed a wide variation in size of these brain nuclei in gay and straight men, but there was still a broad overlap between straight and gay. What he actually found was a distributional difference, with a few larger-than-average nuclei at one end, a few smaller-than-average nuclei at the other, and the vast majority falling in between. Even if we could say most people at one extreme were straight, and most at the other extreme were gay, that tells us little about the majority in the middle where the ranges overlap. If LeVay picked a nucleus size in the middle, he couldn't tell if it was heterosexual or homosexual." See Nimmons, "Sex and the Brain," pp. 64–67.

All of these problems confirm the biblical view that homosexuality is a behavior which, although perhaps more likely in some than others, is not determined but learned. Some research backs this view up directly. For example, Finkelhor (1981), in his study of college students, did find that boys victimized by older men were four times more likely to be currently engaged in homosexual activity than were nonvictims. See Mark Williams, "Father Son Incest: A Review and Analysis of Reported Incidents," *Clinical Social Work Journal*, Vol. 16 (Summer 1988), pp. 165–179. In another study, the researcher reported on eight of his clients who were sexually abused as children by males. Of the eight, six identified themselves as being homosexual, one heterosexual continuously questioned his sexual orientation, and the other heterosexual expressed extreme homophobia. See Martin Schwartz, "Negative Impact of Sexual Abuse on Adult Male Gender: Issues and Strategies of Intervention," *Child and Adolescent Social Work Journal*, Vol. 11 (November 3, 1994), pp. 179–195. These findings accord with our own experience. A large proportion of homosexuals either were abused by men or engaged in preteen sexual experimentation with another male, probably resulting in learned homosexual orientation. Interestingly, little study has been done on the relationship—well known to social workers, counselors, and pastors—between child sexual abuse, incest, and homosexuality. This subject is politically improper in today's climate.

ELEVEN

OVERCOMING OBSTACLES FROM THE PAST:
ADDICTIONS, MATERIALISM, AND PSYCHOLOGICAL DAMAGE

If mates "change" after marriage, it is only in the direction they were already headed, not in the direction that the other may have hoped for.

—SYDNEY HARRIS

In the previous chapter we discussed the importance of resolving relational problems incurred in the past. This chapter examines other past problems and their impact on marriage.

Substance Abuse

Many who are considering marriage spent some time involved in the drug culture. Former addicts or frequent abusers of drugs, including alcohol, need to gain control of these problems before they can expect healthy dating and marriage.

Those with a history of substance abuse often have difficulty forming deep and consistent relationships. This is true for several reasons. First, involvement in drug or alcohol abuse at an early age tends to impair the relational development that

153

should take place during late childhood, adolescence, and early adulthood. Instead of learning how to interact with people in a mature way, substance abusers engage in pseudo-relating based on partying and silly talk, most of which they can't remember later.

Some drugs can deliver a feeling of closeness with party friends, even when no actual closeness exists. The result is devastating when it comes to relational skills. The task of building friendships is often hard work, and while we would not suggest that there is no place for silly talk or partying, these are not the main foundation for relationship beyond the shallowest level. Substance abusers who have constant access to counterfeit closeness find it quite difficult to enter into the much more demanding and painful work of building mature relationships, especially marriages. Their growth in relational ability was simply arrested at the point in time when they began using drugs.

Chronic abuse at any age will impair people's ability to form deep relationships. Indeed, some become involved in drug or alcohol abuse *because* of relational problems. The drugs serve as a temporary but convenient escape from the pressures of everyday life. Drugs and alcohol can also substitute for the kind of stimulation and fulfillment that good relationships can provide. In a word, though abusers may have no close relationships, they manage to escape the pain of loneliness temporarily. No wonder drugs are detrimental to the process of maturing, which includes facing difficult situations and building healthy relationships.

In order to build a relationship that will sustain the pressures of marriage, people need to be free from drug abuse. This does not mean merely breaking the chronic drug-use habit; it means they are not getting intoxicated *at all*.[1] Even after users cease taking drugs, they may retain the habit of escaping rather than resolving problems. Ex-users need to demonstrate the ability to relate consistently and resolve interpersonal problems before they can expect healthy marriages. Any deficiencies in this area should be weighed when considering whether to wait for more maturity before marrying, or to move ahead with marriage at the present time.

What practical steps will help one who still has problems with substance abuse? Consider the following suggestions.

- You may have to avoid old friends who are still involved in substance abuse unless they agree to abstain when around you. If you are still struggling with addictive tendencies, you cannot expect self-control when partying with these people. Perhaps the day will come later when you can return to spend time with these friends and share with them how you gained your freedom.
- If you fall into temptation and become intoxicated again, you should confess the episode to close friends or to your spouse. This helps to negatively reinforce the experience of intoxication, and it interrupts the secrecy so important to some types of addiction. Failure to admit falling creates a sense of alienation from others ("If they only knew!") which in turn tends to aggravate the temptation to get intoxicated again.
- Diligently apply yourself to building a lifestyle based on spiritual growth, fellowship, relationships, and ministry. The stimulation provided by substance abuse must be *replaced* by the righteous stimulation that comes from godly living if you want lasting change. (See 2 Timothy 2:22 for one of many passages that teach this "resist/replace" principle.)
- At the earliest sign that you are losing self-control, seek professional help or the help of Christian friends who understand your problem. You do far better to seek such help *before* a serious relapse costs you ground already gained in sobriety, as well as trust in your key relationships.

Materialism

Materialism is more than just a crass worship of money and things. It is a subtle and sophisticated worldview that defines identity, fulfillment, significance, and security in terms of economics.[2] Ask a materialist who he is, and the first thing that comes into his mind is how he accumulates money and things: "I'm an engineer." Ask him how secure he is in regard to the future, and he will answer in monetary terms: "I have $5,000 in savings, $25,000 in investments, and a $150,000 IRA." Ask him about the goals for his life, and he will answer again in financial terms: career advancement, increased salary, investments and possessions, and, of course, retirement goals.

Though some claim that we live in a "Judeo-Christian" society, materialism is clearly the dominant value system in the modern West. Media, the business world, and much of public education insist that economic progress is more important than spiritual and moral progress. We are constantly reminded of the need for financial security, but rarely or never reminded of the need to deal decisively with eternal issues. Those missing or ignoring opportunities for spiritual progress because they "have to work" are considered responsible. Those who forfeit career advancement for the sake of "spiritual commitments" are considered fanatical and in need of deprogramming.

Materialism is a philosophy of disappointment. Its disciples are inevitably victimized by appealing but false promises of fulfillment and security. But people cannot be truly satisfied by impersonal, material objects, or by temporarily heightened status.

> Materialism is a philosophy of disappointment.

Thus, the endless variety of materialistic goals such as houses, cars, vacations, wardrobes, and entertainment only temporarily satiate our appetites, while leaving untouched our growing inner hunger. As a result, we seek more materialistic stimulation, often leading to a frenzied pursuit of something we can never attain.

Many people spend their lives running down these blind alleys, hoping to fill the void. Finally, after a lifetime of disappointing anticlimaxes, they may become cynical about the possibility of inner contentment and may even deny its existence.

We all must die. This obvious inevitability exposes materialism as a cruel sham, since material possessions can neither prevent death nor be taken into the next life. (See Luke 12:15–21 and 1 Timothy 6:7.) But materialistic lust *can* distract us from thinking about our spiritual and eternal needs and how to deal with them. Materialism is a spiritual harlot, offering satisfaction it can never deliver and distracting us from the only One who can.

Even true Christians, when seduced by materialism, are robbed of the joy of real spiritual fruitfulness. In their case, the "thorns and thistles" which are "the worries of the world, and the deceitfulness of riches, and the desires for other things enter in and choke the word, and it becomes unfruitful" (Mark 4:19). When Christian leaders reinforce these materialistic values instead of confronting them, tragedy is compounded.

How can we know if we are controlled by materialistic values? Most Christians admit that it's possible to be materialistic, and that certain other Christians *are* materialistic, but few acknowledge that *they themselves* are materialistic here and now. However, materialism must be a chronic temptation for most Christians since the Bible warns us against it so often. (See Matthew 6:19–24; 1 John 2:15–17; James 4:1–4; and 1 Timothy 6:7–10.) Some reflective questions may help us recognize where our thinking needs help in this area.

> Materialism is a spiritual harlot, offering satisfaction it can never deliver and distracting us from the only One who can.

- Do you experience conflict between materialistic and spiritual desires? Scripture teaches that this conflict is *normal* for Christians (Galatians 5:17) and is actually a sign of spiritual *health*. If we cannot identify a battle within ourselves over values in the area of materialism, it suggests that we have substantially given in to our fallen nature in this area.

157

- What makes up your private fantasies of the "ideal life"? Are they dominated by new cars and stereos, beautiful homes, professional prestige, world travel, hobby pursuits, early retirement, and financial security? Honest reflection may reveal that spiritual growth and service are just one aspect of this ideal life rather than being its cornerstone and goal. If this is the case, we are enmeshed in a materialistic mind-set.

- How do you *habitually* respond when spiritual and secular responsibilities conflict? We all have more demands placed on us than we can fulfill. We all fail to meet some demands that we would like to have met. The question is, when we are in such situations, which demands do we normally meet, and from which ones do we excuse ourselves? Invariably, our true value system will be expressed by the pattern of our choices in this area. Not only will we cut the demands that we deem less important, but we will follow our real value system when doing so rather than the one we hold out to others (and even to ourselves) as "spiritual." If we find that spiritual growth and ministry opportunities are habitually jettisoned whenever school or work or recreation calls, this indicates that we value these things more than spiritual growth and ministry. In other words, it indicates that we are materialistic.

- Are you able to be content with what you have materially? Do you consciously distinguish between "wants" and "needs"? Are you consistently able to resist buying "wants" when it would compromise your giving or your budget? How much debt have you accumulated from unnecessary acquisitions?

- How regularly and generously do you give your money to God's service? Are you a sporadic giver? Do you only give out of what is left over after other acquisitions? Which direction are you moving in this area?

- What are your short-term and long-term goals? Do you have spiritual goals of both sorts? Or are your goals only career and material goals?

- Are you excited about God, and do you have a clear critique of materialism? Are you seeing new ways that materialism robs people of abundant life? Or has your excitement about God become cool, and has your critique of materialism become vague and filled with unnecessary qualifications?
- How do you view retirement? Is it a time to focus on material enjoyment that you have earned, or is it a time of greater freedom to serve God?

Many Christians have a carefully woven line drawn through their lives that says, "Christ has a say up to this point, but no farther." Maybe the line is drawn just before career advancement or dating or hobbies or leisure time. When Christian involvement encroaches on these things, they say no. Maybe the line is drawn at the kind of people with whom they are willing to relate. If ministry opportunities demand working with an unsophisticated person, they politely refuse. Such resistance may occur in many other areas, but the existence of such a line reveals a value system tainted with materialism.

Marriage and Materialism

Materialism is a direct menace to a God-centered marriage. But ironically, both Scripture and experience agree that marriage tends to *increase* materialistic temptation. In 1 Corinthians 7:32–34, Paul says:

> One who is unmarried is concerned about the things of the Lord, how he may please the Lord; but one who is married is concerned about the things of the world, how he may please his wife . . . [or], how she may please her husband.

But this is Paul's observation, not his wish. Unfortunately, the observation is still as true today as when it was written. Paul is so against this tendency that he goes on to imply that if marriage is going to result in fixation on the world system, we should consider staying single. This is why, in the same passage, Paul also says,

... brethren, the time has been shortened, so that from now on ... those who have wives should be as though they had none ... and those who buy, as though they did not possess; and those who use the world, as though they did not make full use of it (1 Corinthians 7:29–31).

This passage uses the figure of speech known as *hyberbole*—deliberate exaggeration to make a point. Paul clearly taught that getting married is never a reason to drop out of active personal ministry.

Both marriage and children necessitate more involvement with and attention to financial matters. Greater attention to these matters is legitimate, especially when children arrive. But God wants us to learn to "walk and chew gum at the same time." We should be able to make responsible material provision for our family while maintaining a firm commitment to spiritual priorities. Instead, many Christian couples gradually wane in their commitment to Christ in this stage of life and never recover that commitment later on.

The impact of materialism on marriage can be substantial. Not only can our focus drift from Christ to money, but we also may find ourselves accepting a destructive level of absenteeism for one or both spouses based on the pursuit of more money and "success." The truth is, we are not succeeding at all. We may very well be destroying our marriage and our children's experience of their family and parents for no good reason. Our pleas that "we only want what is best for them" may be a thin veil of deception covering our misdirected, selfish ambition.

> Christian marriage is not to be a cozy nest safely insulated from the needs of others.

Materialism has a very enmeshing effect on people. The more we slip into materialism, the more we come to believe we need just a bit more simply to maintain what we already have. Things we once viewed as unnecessary luxuries have a way of becoming necessities. Christian couples should soberly reflect on this tendency to pursue "personal peace and affluence" once they get married and the children arrive.[3] Only firm biblical convictions in this area coupled with a lifestyle of spiritual growth and service will counteract this tendency.

Engaged Christian couples are usually advised to reach agreement with each other about life-goals and priorities. This advice is good. But it's often implied (and sometimes openly stated) that a materialistic lifestyle is okay as long as both agree on this value system! Nothing could be further from the biblical ideal for marriage. Christian marriage is not to be a cozy nest safely insulated from the needs of others. It is to be a sacrificial love relationship that not only builds up husband, wife, and children, but also brings healing to those outside the family unit.[4]

Resisting Materialism

Christians should consciously and emphatically reject materialism. Scripture views materialistic lust as idolatry. (See Colossians 3:5: ". . . consider the members of your earthly body as dead to . . . greed, which amounts to idolatry.") Our identity, fulfillment, and security should come from our relationship with God and fulfilling the purpose he has for our lives. In Ephesians 2:10 Paul says, ". . . we are his workmanship, created in Christ Jesus for good works, which God prepared beforehand, that we should walk in them." Our life goals and direction should be based on God's will for us, including the people whom he gives us opportunity to serve. (See Matthew 6:19–21, 23; and 1 Thessalonians 2:19–20.) For all of these reasons, materialism as a value system is absolutely incompatible with Christianity.

We should view money and possessions not only as a gift from God for our needs and enjoyment, but also as a stewardship to be used for the needs of others. (See Ephesians 4:28 and 2 Corinthians 8:13–15.)

Since materialism is such a formidable foe, consider the following practical suggestions for resisting it.

- Establish the habit of sacrificially giving to God's work. This giving should represent a significant portion of our income rather than an amount that we "feel" we should give. (See 1 Corinthians 16:2.) Impulsive giving falls short of the biblical ideal, which is based on commitment, not momentary feeling or sentimentality. Our giving should be "off the top" rather than from what we have left over after buying other things. Jesus teaches us that where we invest our money dictates where our heart follows. (See Luke 12:34.) As income increases, seriously consider the "graduated tithe" as outlined by Ronald J. Sider in *Rich Christians in an Age of Hunger* (Downers Grove, Ill.: InterVarsity Press, 1984), pp. 162–177.
- Establish a vital personal ministry. (See Chapter 6.) Nothing helps to resist the temptation to succumb to materialism like the satisfaction of being used by God to serve other people for Christ. Unfortunately, the opposite is also true. Nothing makes us ineffective in ministry more quickly than the onset of materialism. Decide beforehand that you will be consistent in ministry even if it means missing chances to make money and advance in your career.
- Resist the tendency to seek love feelings from materialistic stimulation such as buying binges, expensive recreation habits, etc. Instead, cultivate a taste for recreation that emphasizes personal interaction with others. Such recreation is not only cheaper, but also more rewarding and beneficial.

Psychological Damage

A number of psychological problems could call into question plans for marriage. The following areas raise special concern:

- chronic or clinical depression
- anxiety attacks
- phobias

- eating disorders
- nervous breakdowns
- acute schizophrenic or bipolar episodes
- personality disorders

Any of these problems are serious enough to give pause to marriage plans. Any one could damage or even destroy a marriage. On the other hand, if we have our psychological problems under control, they need not affect marriage plans. Just be sure you have shared any past problems with your prospective spouse. Also, seek professional counsel when assessing the seriousness of one of these problems. Only when our problems are sufficiently under control should we view marriage as a feasible short-term goal rather than a longer-term goal.

Summing Up

Clearly, Christians need not wait until they are engaged to address these problem areas. By walking with Christ, we can see substantial relational healing regardless of our marital status. The time to accept the challenge of allowing God to heal us is while we are still uninvolved in a serious romantic relationship. If we make progress now, we will experience much easier adjustment later on when we do become seriously involved.

Notes

1. Ephesians 5:18 states that Christians should "not get drunk with wine, for that is dissipation." Galatians 5:20 lists *pharmakeia* ("sorcery") as one of the deeds of the flesh to be avoided. *Pharmakeia* refers not only to sorcery, but also to the mixing of potions and thus encompasses drug use for the purpose of mind alteration. 1 Thessalonians 5:6 says that we should be "alert and sober" in contrast to those who "get drunk."
2. Technically, materialism is the philosophical position that nothing other than matter exists. But we are using the word in its more popular sense of "avarice," or basing one's life on the values of material wealth.
3. For an excellent critique of materialism, see Francis A. Schaeffer, *How Should We Then Live?* (Old Tappan, N.J.: Fleming H. Revell Co., 1976), pp. 205–227; and *No Little People* (Downers Grove, Ill.: InterVarsity Press, 1975), pp. 257–271.
4. Notice that in the epistles, Christians are consistently addressed as members of the Body of Christ *before* they are addressed as spouses. This implies that our identity as Christians is the foundation upon which we are to build our identity as spouses. As such, our responsibility to sacrificially serve others in the church and in the world is assumed as an element and purpose of Christian marriage. See Ephesians 4:17–5:33 and Colossians 3:1–19 for examples of this order.

TWELVE
PERSONAL MATURITY

It is not marriage that fails; it is the people that fail. All that marriage does is to show people up.

—H. E. FOSDICK

The first thing to be done by a biographer in estimating character is to examine the stubs of the victim's checkbooks.

—SILAS W. MITCHELL

Marriage requires maturity. The more mature both partners are, the better the prospects for any marriage. We need to consider maturity in both the spiritual and emotional areas of life.

Spiritual Maturity

Spiritual maturity takes time. The Bible uses the metaphor of "growth" to describe our development of spiritual maturity, and growth is a gradual process. (See Ephesians 4:15; 1 Peter 2:2; and 2 Peter 3:18.) Although having been a Christian for six years does not guarantee spiritual maturity, no one is spiritually mature after six months. Therefore, if possible, we need to consider logging some time growing as Christians before we get married. Of course, there could be other factors that might make early marriage the best choice even for young Christians, as we shall see.

Spiritual maturity is the result of sufficient time spent ac-

tively growing in our relationship with Christ. This process includes not only a personal prayer life, but also laying a foundation of biblical knowledge, developing solid Christian
relationships, and learning to serve others in the power of the
Spirit. Maturity also requires that we have suffered trials under
the healing discipline of God as he brings to light damage in
our character and works to correct it. (See Hebrews 12:11–13.)

Factors in Spiritual Growth

The rate at which we grow spiritually depends on a variety
of factors, including:

- our willingness to cooperate with God;
- the seriousness of our personal problems at the time we
  came to Christ;
- the amount and quality of help we receive from others in
  our Christian environment.

However, even when our growth is rapid, time is necessary.
Attaining spiritual maturity requires years, not months. The
apostle Paul suggests that substantial spiritual maturity is possible within two to four years after coming to Christ. He wrote
to the Corinthians two to four years after they came to Christ
and was disappointed that they were still babies in the faith. He
expected them to have a measure of maturity in that time. (See
1 Corinthians 3:1–3.)

If possible, we would do well to delay the decision to get
married until we have attained a good measure of spiritual maturity. Some have succeeded in building successful marriages
even though they were very young Christians. Others come to
Christ already married and must develop spiritual maturity
within marriage. While this is possible, it is not optimal. Often,
spiritual immaturity causes serious marital problems (sometimes even resulting in divorce), which probably could have
been avoided if the couple had greater maturity at the outset.
For instance, many of the concepts of self-sacrifice discussed
earlier may seem strange and unrealistic to the spiritually im-

mature. Maybe this is why we never find a happily married Christian couple who regret having waited for additional maturity before getting married. However, we find many who wished they had waited longer.

Problems could also develop from too much waiting. For instance, sexual pressure may become a barrier to further spiritual growth. Each couple must weigh, hopefully with the help of mature counsel, the trade-off of values and dangers.

Spiritual Maturity in You: Proven Endurance

You cannot be sure your spiritual growth is genuine unless it continues through adversity. The Bible says God uses adversity to build our faith and develop maturity. In James 1:2–4, we are admonished to, "Consider it all joy, my brethren, when you encounter various trials, knowing that the testing of your faith produces endurance. And let endurance have its perfect result, that you may be perfect and complete, lacking in nothing." Suffering can strengthen your resolve to follow God and can accomplish changes in your character as long as you respond in the right way.

Loneliness is one type of trial common to single Christians. God may call you to experience an extended time without any romantic relationships. This is especially likely if you have been excessively dependent on romance for the bulk of your love feelings, or if you have other problems that might inhibit a mature dating relationship. (See Chapters 9 and 10.) Christians who struggle against God's loving discipline in this area may turn to illegitimate pain reducers, which could short-circuit the growth process. If, on the other hand, we learn during such trials what God is trying to teach us about ourselves and what it means to depend on him, his discipline will have the desired effect. We can then approach serious dating and marriage with a tested dependence on Christ.

The ability to walk with God consistently without involvement in a romantic relationship is a definite sign of maturity. But if you grow resentful and frantically strive to find a dating relationship, allowing the rest of your walk to deteriorate, you are demonstrating immaturity.

This ties in with an earlier thought. Marriage is a good goal, but how is that goal obtained? There is nothing wrong with dating or searching for a mate, but many need to put less emphasis on seeking out a person to marry, and focus more on developing their own character so that they will be prepared for marriage when God grants them a mate.

When the desire for marriage becomes obsessive, it ironically becomes a barrier to achieving the goal of a godly marriage. God may then ask you to surrender your demands to him and entrust this area of your life to his timing and wisdom. One sign that you have done so would be an inner relaxation and gratitude that results from trusting God.

> When the desire for marriage becomes obsessive, it ironically becomes a barrier to achieving the goal of a godly marriage.

You may still experience loneliness and the desire to be married, but these will be tempered by confidence in God's willingness to help you in this area. You are then liberated to concentrate more on maturing spiritually and on serving others.

Spiritual Maturity in Your Mate

You should also be willing to wait for a mate who is reasonably mature spiritually. This may not always be possible, but you are taking chances if you decide to marry an immature Christian. Are you willing to lose a few dates because you refuse to develop a romantic relationship with a spiritually immature person? If not, you are running a significant risk, and you can expect problems.

Too often, Christians select a partner who has pleasing physical features, and then hope that person will decide to commit to spiritual growth. Such a plan may work, but the failures outnumber the successes. Why not accept God's priorities as your own?

I'm Already Married!

For those who are already engaged or married, the pressure to grow spiritually is greater, not less. Married people need to realize that their own spiritual growth is God's solution for their problems in marriage. Many couples in distressed marriages have fought their way through to victory when they were willing to put Christ first and grow in him. Christian marriage counseling may also be necessary, but not even the best Christian counselor can make others mature spiritually.

Likewise, engaged couples should realize that the short time left to them before marriage is a unique opportunity. Normally, engaged couples worry about things such as arranging the marriage ceremony, choosing the china pattern, and picking out flowers. Though perhaps necessary and reasonable, none of these things actually matter when it comes to the vitality of their marriage. Most would do well to resist the societal pressure to focus on materialistic issues, and instead commit some time to advancing in spiritual growth. Although there is no reason to needlessly offend family and friends, don't base your wedding on the "lust of the eyes and the boastful pride of life" (see 1 John 2:16). Christians should set spiritual growth as their top priority and carry out the other preparations for the wedding day as they are able.

Chronological Age

According to divorce statistics, most urban young people today would do well to delay marriage until their twenties. There are, of course, exceptions to this general maxim. Some people mature more quickly, especially if they were raised in stable families and if they have been vital Christians for years. Others are unable to delay for a number of reasons. However, the evidence shows that few teenagers today are likely to succeed at marriage.[1] The most obvious reason why teenage marriages fail so often (whether Christian or non-Christian) is the lack of emotional maturity.

In biblical times, couples usually married in their mid-teens. However, this should not be considered normative for today for two obvious reasons. First, the decision then of when and whom to marry was in the hands of older, mature people—namely, their parents. Most of us would not be willing to let our parents pick our life-partners so that we could get married sooner!

Second, new pressures, unimagined in the ancient world, confront the married couple today. Western concepts of moral relativism, the need for constant romantic feelings, materialism, family disintegration, and the ease of divorce combine to bombard new marriages. So also does the high level of sexual titillation in Western dress, the mass media, and various types of pornography. Such an environment is quite different from that of young people in ancient Jewish culture who often reached adulthood without ever seeing a member of the opposite sex outside their family even partially nude. Agrarian couples also usually lived with the extended family, receiving support and counsel in a way few modern couples do.

Christian couples today cannot expect the same cultural support in their marriage that their biblical counterparts received. Rather, they must have enough maturity in themselves to discern and effectively combat the cultural pressures present in today's world.

Emotional Maturity

As we have noted, emotional maturity is the missing component in most youthful marriages. One index of such maturity is what could be called *functional responsibility*. Consider the following questions:

- Am I always changing jobs?
- Am I perpetually dissatisfied with the job I have?
- Do I have trouble holding a job?

If the answer to these questions is yes, there is a lack of functional responsibility. Such a deficiency puts an unnecessary strain on marriage.

The same is true of fiscal management. Those who find themselves chronically in excessive debt and unable to control their spending probably need more time to develop basic self-control and maturity. Inability to hold a job or manage money will exert excessive pressures on a marriage.

Faithful in Little, Faithful in Much

Christ teaches that if we are not responsible in the small areas of life, neither will we be responsible in the major areas. (See Luke 16:10–12.) This is why the mundane things, such as our jobs and how we handle our money, are so significant. We need to learn responsibility so we can present ourselves to our spouse as a suitable mate, not a baby-sitting project.

We are not suggesting that Christians adopt the secular idea of "success" as a criterion for marriage. According to this view, young people should hoard unnecessary wealth in order to prove their worthiness. Those who are able to flaunt their consumption show they are ready for marriage. Nothing could be further from the biblical picture of marriage. According to the Bible, Christians should be content to live a simple life and "eat their own bread" (2 Thessalonians 3:12). A Christian who hoards unnecessary wealth is demonstrating serious value problems and identity problems. Generosity is a better indication of worthiness in a Christian.

If you are already married and your marriage is afflicted with functional irresponsibility, you may need to seek out a mature Christian financial counselor. Such a counselor can teach you the principles of fiscal responsibility and help you set up a budget. It is an act of sacrificial love when you show the willingness to swallow your pride and seek outside help for the sake of your marriage. Again and again, couples have later rejoiced that they took such problems in hand.

Notes

1. According to the National Center for Health Statistics, women married at ages 14–17 had three times the probability, and women married at ages 18–19 had twice the probability of being divorced as had women married at ages 20–24. *Teenage Marriage and Divorce: United States, 1970–81* (Hyattsville, Md.: U.S. Department of Health and Human Services, Public Health Service, National Center for Health Statistics, 1985), p. 13. In fairness, these statistics have not been controlled for Christian versus non-Christian teens. Our experience shows that Christian teen marriages do better than those of non-Christians, but they clearly have far more problems than Christians who marry when older.

THIRTEEN

A Fulfilling Marriage *Is* Possible!

Society creates the myth that marriage is the proper haven for all our longings and a cure for all our shortcomings. People are programmed to believe that marriage will automatically give them individuality, identity, security, and happiness, when as a matter of fact marriage gives them none of these things unless they possess them in the first place.

—Gerald Griffin

No one meets all of the criteria discussed in this book in any absolute sense. However, many Christian couples have invested enough time and effort to gain relative success in all of these areas. Those who do this *before* getting married can be the most assured of success in marriage. Even within marriage, those couples who commit themselves to work toward maturity in these areas can count on a more fulfilling marriage.

Specific or Broad-based Maturity?

Some people think their outstanding strength in one area will counter their serious failure in another. However, married couples find that the absence of even one of these criteria is surprisingly damaging to their marriages. For instance, you may be an outstanding Christian minister but have never developed sexual self-control. Or you may have a deep prayer life but have never developed close personal relationships. Such scenarios are dangerous. It would be much better to see some progress in all of the areas we have covered than to see great development in some areas with little development in others. A consistent, broad-based maturity is better than specialized strength.

Where Are You Headed?

Another important issue is your direction, or movement, in the areas we have discussed. Are you cooperating with God in the resolution of your remaining problems, or are you stagnating? As Christians, we rarely can say that our problems in any area have been totally resolved. But we can say that they *are* being resolved, or that they have been *substantially* resolved. If we have a problem, we should be able to say that we are taking steps to overcome it, and that we are already seeing results. This proactive, diligent attitude toward our spiritual growth is indispensable. (See 2 Peter 1:4–10.)

We should also feel hope when we cultivate the expectation that God will continue to transform our lives as we have seen him doing since we began to cooperate with him. (See Philippians 1:6.) Such hope is extremely helpful, especially in distressed marriages.

No Legalism, Please!

It is sadly possible to approach the concepts in this book according to the "letter" and not according to the spirit. In other words, some will attempt to perform external actions only as a means to get what they want: immediate marriage or immediate relief from marital pain. Such an approach would be a complete waste of time and effort. We need to honestly take these issues up with God. He truly wants what is best for our lives. He really does know how to bring about the changes needed for our happiness, and he is willing and able to make those changes if we have the trust and the patience to cooperate with him.

174

Your Outlook

Are romance, love, and marriage important to you? If so, why settle for less than the best? Is there any good reason why you shouldn't attain relative maturity in all of the areas we have discussed? Why not make a personal commitment to this effect between you and God?

Wouldn't it be nice to have strong assurance that your marriage will succeed? With the patience and faith from your side to cooperate with God while he works on your character from his side, you can expect an exciting future in marriage. With your enhanced relational capability, your deepened knowledge of the Word of God, your established habit of spiritual sharing with your prospective spouse, your personal competence in ministry, and the support of your local church, you can face marriage with the confidence that you are about to launch into a wonderful phase of your life.

> Are romance, love, and marriage important to you? If so, why settle for less than the best?

Such assurance is not only possible; it is God's will. While nothing is completely without risk in this life, Christians who follow these recommendations can rest assured that their marriages will almost certainly succeed. You will have problems. But you will also have the tools you need to appropriate God's wisdom and power to solve those problems.

"Love (*agape*) never fails . . ." (1 Corinthians 13:8). What an exciting and secure future we have within God's will!

For more material on marriage and dating including a free study guide for *The Myth of Romance*, call 1–800–698–7884, or visit *The Myth of Romance* page at http://www.xenos.org/myth.html. You can also ask the authors a question or leave a comment at that World Wide Web page.